Table of Contents

Section/Chapter

Section 1		3
Section 2	...ay of Thinking	108
Section 3	Overcoming Depression	136

How to Stay Out

Chapter 1	Al's Story	3
Chapter 2	Why Al Failed	5
Chapter 3	Change	7
Chapter 4	How We Build Our Brain	8
Chapter 5	Our Self Image	10
Chapter 6	Social Acceptance	15
Chapter 7	Making Friends	16
Chapter 8	Cause and Effect	16
Chapter 9	A Normal Family	20
Chapter 10	Free Will	20
Chapter 11	Support	21
Chapter 12	Leo's Story	24
Chapter 13	Leo's Plan	27
Chapter 14	Emotions	27
Chapter 15	Unseen Scars	32
Chapter 16	Self Destructive Behavior	33
Chapter 17	Donardo's Story	35
Chapter 18	SDB as Revenge	38
Chapter 19	The Uniqueness of Our Lives	39
Chapter 20	Juan's Story	40
Chapter 21	Changing Our Self Image	43
Chapter 22	Subconscious Instructions	47
Chapter 23	Juan's Image	48
Chapter 24	Juan's Plan	50
Chapter 25	Mantra	52
Chapter 26	Self Destructive Behavior II	54

Chapter 27	Controlling Our SDB	56
Chapter 28	SDB III	57
Chapter 29	Juan's Final Plan	62
Chapter 30	John's Story	63
Chapter 31	Turning Things Around	68
Chapter 32	Donardo's Story	69
Chapter 33	Addiction	70
Chapter 34	Control versus Rules	71
Chapter 35	George's Story	73
Chapter 36	Guilt	75
Chapter 37	Al's Self Image	79
Chapter 38	Improving Our Thinking	80
Chapter 39	Positive Thinking	81
Chapter 40	Changing Beliefs	82
Chapter 41	Financial Maturity	87
Chapter 42	Donardo's Plan	88
Chapter 43	Amnesty	90
Chapter 44	Judging	92
Chapter 45	Al's Plan	94
Chapter 46	Leo's Success	95
Chapter 47	Anxiety	96
Chapter 48	George's Plan	99
Chapter 49	The NA Group Ends	101
Chapter 50	Success	102
Chapter 51	Donardo's Letters	103
Chapter 52	George's Letters	103
Chapter 53	Juan's Letters	105
Chapter 54	Al's Letters	106

Renewal Center Publishing
Copyright © 2011, Brownsville TX
All rights reserved.

How to Stay Out

The good news is – you are going to get out. The bad news is, without a good plan and a lot of hard work, you are probably coming back. Let's look at Al's story in his own words:

Chapter 1 – Al's Story

I grew up in a dysfunctional home where love was scarce and abuse rampant. I only felt the warmth of my mother's touch when I grabbed her, as I begged her to stop beating me. She was always calling me names, like "sad dog" and "dummy." I never knew my dad.

I think I was five when I ran away and lived with my grandpa. His love was the only haven in my life of hell. He was good to me and believed in me.

I was six when a neighbor lured me into his lust, promising me toys. When I discovered the truth, I was covered in shame – but never told anyone.

That same year my grandpa died of cancer. He was the only good thing in my world, and he was gone. I had to go back with my mother. But her anger and venom increased each year, and after a violent beating, I decided to be out of the house whenever she was there.

I hit the streets, full of anger and hate. I started drinking at 10, then into drugs at 12. I started committing crime, even stealing from my mother. By my early teens I was in juvenile hall, which led to Texas Youth Camp and so on, until I ended up in the Cameron County Jail.

In jail I met a group of fellows whose lives mirrored my own. But they had found an identity – gang affiliation. They painted a beautiful picture of loyalty, love and purpose, and my desperate heart shouted, "Yes!" When I got out, I went to work for them. I sold cocaine – used it too. But I was caught, and spent five years in prison.

As I sat in my cell day after day it became obvious to me that gangs would mean a life in prison. So I left the gang. It wasn't easy, but I decided to go straight. When I got out, I got a job working for an A/C company and, at the same time, started buying and selling used cars. Our A/C company had a baseball team, and I was invited to play. One of the other players also played on a soccer team, and I joined that team, too. I enjoyed playing sports and making new friends. I was getting in good shape and starting to feel good about myself.

But for some reason, this good feeling worried me. The more I succeeded, the more I worried. It was like I didn't deserve this success. I had this recurring fear that one day I would turn back into my old self – the "real" me – the addict, the drug dealer, the convict.

These thoughts haunted and confused me, and I started back on cocaine. As I laid my first line I remember shouting, "What's wrong with me?" But I did it anyway. That got me hooked, and each day I needed a little more. My habit ate all my money, and my life started to crumble. I needed a fix, but I was broke. My pusher told me he'd give me a week of crack if I drove him for a drive-by shooting. "No," I said, "I don't do that anymore." But I needed the fix, so we took my car. I stopped in front of the house, he blasted the house with 8 bullets, and we drove off – but not fast enough. A neighbor got my license number, and here I am – in prison again.

What's wrong with me? I had it all and threw it away. How could I do something so stupid? I'm stupid, I'm junk, I'm garbage, and I deserve to be here. I deserve the worst they can give me. What's wrong with me?

Chapter 2 – Why Al Failed

Al's story is not unusual. It is quite common for people with a history of abuse, drugs and crime to make incredibly poor decisions. When he looked back at his decision he labeled himself stupid. But actually Al was intelligent. When he was in school, he did well. As an adult he learned A/C installation in a year, and ran a successful used car business. He played sports, made new friends and was on the road to success. Why then did he destroy it all? He knew drugs and violence were wrong, but he returned to them anyway. Why?

Al had a very negative childhood. He had been sexually abused, physically abused and pushed away by his mother. We all have negative things that happen to us as children, and our minds soak up all this negativity like little sponges. These events sit in our subconscious and, if they are bad enough, can affect our emotions when we become adults. It's probable that Al carried a lot of "emotional baggage" into adulthood. The abuse and rejection he received as a child caused him to feel shameful and unworthy, and he started to see himself negatively. The loss of his grandfather drove him to rebel against anything good. The guilt from his delinquency and his time locked up all added to his negative self image. So as an adult, when he started being successful, his subconscious compared his success with his negative self image, and he felt he didn't deserve the success.

Our human brains are complicated. If we carry around a lot of guilt, then we might destroy the things we feel we don't deserve. If all we have known is negatives, then we feel uncomfortable with positives. For every person who is afraid of failure, there is at least one person who is afraid of success. Possibly, Al felt if he succeeded, then others would expect him to continue to succeed, and that was too much pressure. Something inside told him it was easier to fail. He was good at it.

Al is not alone. Thousands of smart people damage and destroy their lives every day. Every year, hundreds of thousands of inmates leave incarceration, and then purposely do things that get them re-incarcerated. According to the FBI, two out of three released inmates are back in trouble within 3 years. These statistics seem almost unbelievable, yet we know they are true. And they shout an ironic truth – that it's easier to get out – than to stay out. So the question is, 'What can we do to insure we won't come back here again?' And the answer is, 'Planning.' It is extremely important to have a plan when we get out – a plan that will completely change our lives – a plan that will override all our old bad habits.

When Al left prison he started out on the right track. He left the gang, got an honest job, worked hard, and learned his trade well. He joined sports teams, made new friends, and got in shape. These were all very important things to do in changing his life.

By leaving the gang, he separated himself from those people who were most likely to drag him back into drugs and crime. By joining the sports teams, he started associating with people whose lives were going in a positive direction. His new job gave him an honest way to earn a living. This part of his plan worked well.

But each of us is a product of our past, and therefore we can be influenced by it. If our past is negative, we can be influenced negatively. Al didn't know that he needed to deal with all the negative emotions he carried around with him from both his childhood and his criminal years. These negative emotions were his undoing.

Al didn't realize he needed to change more than just his friends and his job. He needed to change everything; especially his thinking and the way he dealt with his emotions.

And it is the same with all of us when we get out. We can't expect a small change to give us the success we desire. It requires us to change almost every aspect of our past lives. We need to change the way we think, the way we act, the way we feel, the way we present ourselves, our priorities, our goals, our friends, maybe even our families – just about everything. If we are not ready to make major changes, if we are not ready to commit to giving this our best effort, then our chances of success are not good, and we should resign ourselves to a future of incarceration.

The following stories are true. They come from inmates who have agreed to share their past histories. The names have been changed.

Chapter 3 - Change

When we find ourselves incarcerated, we can give up – or we can decide to change. If we commit to change, our attitude will improve, we'll have a goal to shoot for, and our time in jail or prison will pass more quickly.

Al was lucky in a number of ways. First, he was the driver of the car, not the shooter. Second, no one was hurt. So, he was offered a plea deal of four years, which he accepted.

Al spent the first month beating himself up for starting back on drugs and driving the car. But his boss wrote him and told him his job would be waiting for him when he got out. His friends also wrote him supportive letters praising his work, and pointing out how successful he had been at buying and selling used cars. After a while, he also started to see the positive aspects of his life. And one morning he made a commitment to himself that he was going to work even harder this time while in prison to change his life.

Al was also lucky that he was sent to a prison that had counseling that included both Alcoholics Anonymous (AA) and Narcotics Anonymous (NA) issues. He signed up for the counseling and went twice a week. He met four other inmates there, George, Leo, Juan and Donardo. The moderator's name was Bill.

In the beginning, Al was reluctant to talk about his feelings. But after a few meetings, he started to participate. He brought up many of his old memories and how he felt about the abuse and neglect he had received. He talked about how wonderful his grandfather had been and how devastated he was when he died.

Chapter 4 - How We Build Our Brain

Al described the day he fell back into drugs and shouted to himself, "What's wrong with me?" He asked the moderator, Bill, "How could I have made such a poor decision?"

"Well," Bill said, "it may have to do with the way our decision making system develops during childhood. If our childhood is dysfunctional, then our decision making system develops dysfunctionally, and we make poor decisions.

"You see," Bill continued, "when we enter this world, only a small portion of our brain is developed – just enough to allow us to breathe, cry, eat and digest food. The majority of our brain develops as we live life. It develops as we grow and as we learn activities like walking and talking. It develops as we learn skills such as reading and writing. But the cognitive area of our brain, the part that thinks and makes decisions, develops through our experiences with life.

"For example, shortly after birth we feel hunger and start crying. Someone feeds us, and we feel satisfied. Hunger creates crying which brings feeding which causes satisfaction – our thinking structure has started developing. All events that happen to us, such as bathing, diaper changing, recognizing faces, etc., help develop our thinking structure.

"As we get older we get scolded for running in the street, or praised for helping our little sister. This causes our thinking structure to develop. Whether we are dealing with a playground bully, fishing with our dad, or lost in a store searching for our mom, endless experiences occur throughout our childhood, all helping to build our thinking system.

"In effect, our thinking structure is designed by life. But, since life is imperfect and life's ordeals are imperfect, our thinking structure develops imperfectly. The evidence of this is the mistakes we make and the unhappiness we suffer.

"So Al, since most of our thinking structure develops during our youth, and, since your youth was dysfunctional, your thinking structure probably developed dysfunctionally, as did your decision making system. This would explain why you made that poor decision to take drugs. Everyone's thinking system develops imperfectly to some degree. But the more unstable our childhood, the more erratic our decisions will be.

"Our job here in counseling is to discover the imperfections in our thinking system, and to develop tools to overcome them.

Chapter 5 – Our Self Image

"One of the major elements of our thinking system is our self image. It would seem logical, Al, that because of your traumatic youth, your self image developed negatively. So let me ask you, how did you view yourself as a child?"

"Well," Al said, "I remember not having the things the other kids had; they had parents who liked them; they went to movies and the zoo, and got presents at Christmas. I think I was jealous of them, so I tried to get back at them by doing bad things. I destroyed things at school; killed bugs, frogs and lizards; even destroyed my own few toys when I wasn't invited to play with the other kids."

Bill asked, "Did you see yourself as a good person?"

"No," Al said, "Nobody wanted me. I saw myself as an outcast; and I can recall feeling angry about that. So I did bad things and labeled myself the outlaw. But as the bad guy, I was at least somebody – I had an identity."

Bill observed, "It looks like you had a negative self image as a child. You used the word outcast, you saw yourself excluded and rejected?"

"Yes," Al said, "other than my grandfather, no one cared about me, no one wanted me. I felt worthless."

"Self image," Bill explained, "is probably the most important concept in anyone's life. We do not live our lives according to who we are, but who we think we are. We live according to how we perceive ourselves. We act and react as if all of our self perceptions are true. But all of these perceptions are not necessarily true.

"Self-image is nothing more than a collection of ideas we have about ourselves. These ideas are formed in our childhood, and they continue to form throughout our lives. How our parents treat us when we are small affects how we view ourselves as adults. Some of the early ideas we have about ourselves go deep into our subconscious, and we may spend a lifetime trying to change those ideas. But most negative self perceptions are not accurate, and here's why.

"As a child, if an important person, like a parent or teacher, says something negative to us, that negative statement will damage our self image. Al, you're a good example. Your mother was always saying negative things to you, and calling you names. These verbal stings damaged your self image. When your grandfather died, it seemed as if the only person who showed you any love had abandoned you, and that also harmed your self image.

"You perceived yourself as worthless. If you had been raised in a supportive home, you would have been praised for the good things you did, and corrected when you behaved badly. Had that happened, your self image would have been positive. You would have viewed yourself as good and worthwhile. Can you understand, Al, that if you had been raised in a positive environment you would have viewed yourself as worthwhile?"

"Yes," Al said. "That seems logical."

"In reality, you weren't worthless. It was just an image you had of yourself because of your negative childhood experiences.

"Yes," Al said, "I can see that."

"And this also reveals that our self perceptions are not necessarily true. It shows that if we have a negative self image, it might be based on a negative environment, and not because we are actually bad or worthless.

"Most psychologists agree that the foundation of our self image is formed by age five. They also recognize that a negative self image is quite common – that's because it takes 20 positive statements to undo the damage of one negative statement. So if a child hears only one positive statement for every negative statement made, the net result will be bad for his perception of himself. This is because negative comments impact our subconscious far greater than positive ones. Therefore, there are many more negative self images than positive ones, and most of the negative ones are unfounded. Let me ask you, Al, how did you do in school?"

"I did OK," Al said. "When I was there I got mostly B's and C's. But I was always skipping school, so I spent a lot of time in detention."

"Did you ever have a teacher that you felt close to?" Bill asked.

"Not really," Al answered. "They were always upset with me for skipping school and destroying things."

"You see," Bill said, "if there had been a teacher who had taken the time every day to tell you how smart you were, and the evidence was the good grades you were getting, it would have helped undo some of the damage that your self image was receiving at home. Imagine if your mother had said, 'Wow, what a great report card, you sure are smart!' This would have been so much better for you than hearing the word 'dummy'. Unfortunately, most parents are not aware of the damage their words do to their children."

"Is there anything I can do about it?" Al asked.

"You certainly can," Bill said. "Our self-image is a collection of ideas. We can change that image by changing those ideas. We have power over our self image because we can remove those ideas about ourselves, and replace them with new ideas. We can, in effect, rebuild our self image. And we should, because our self image determines the direction of our lives. Many of our actions are driven by our self image; it's who we think we are, and we live according to that perception.

"If a negative self image comes from powerfully traumatic experiences in our childhood, like physical, emotional, or sexual abuse, it takes a lot of courage and self-examination to overcome such an image. Let's look at some examples. Al, you told us previously that you felt like no one cared about you. Could you elaborate on that?"

"Yes," Al said, "my dad deserted us, my mom pushed me away, and my grandpa died. No one wanted me, and I felt worthless. And it seemed like there was nothing I could do about it – except bad things."

"Could you describe the bad things?" Bill asked.

"Well, every time something bad would happen to me, I would feel like taking revenge. Like when everyone else in the neighborhood was having a big Thanksgiving dinner, I had nothing – my mother didn't even come home that day. I was scrounging around in the kitchen looking for something to eat and came across a whole case of beets. My mother loved beets and I hated them, so I threw them all in the garbage. Then I went through the house and found other things that my mother liked and threw them out too."

"How did that make you feel?" Bill asked.

"Well," Al answered, "when I was throwing things away I felt good – it was a rush. But later, I felt bad because I was hurting my mother, and as much as I was mad at her, I still loved her."

"That's understandable," Bill observed.

"One time," Al continued, "two families nearby took all their kids to the beach, and they saw me standing there, and knew I wanted to go, but they just left without asking me. I got mad and thought about throwing a rock through their window. That thought gave me a rush and a good feeling. So I threw the rock through their window. But afterwards I felt bad, like when I broke my own toys and I threw away mom's stuff. I guess I was really mixed up."

Bill asked, "Do you think that the events of your childhood affected your behavior as you grew older? Did you get that rush from doing bad things later in life?"

"Yes I did," Al said. "When I was a teen, I got that same rush when I stole stuff. But it got me sent to Juvie and TYC. And as I got older, I learned I could get that rush from drugs."

Chapter 6 - Social Acceptance

Bill said, "You felt rejected a lot as a child. Do you think that had anything to do with joining a gang as an adult?"

"Now that you mention it," Al answered. "I guess it did. Nobody wanted me as a kid, but the gang treated me like a first class member."

"So," Bill said, "the gang fulfilled your childhood wish for social acceptance."

"Yes," Al said, "yes it did."

"Let's talk about that for a moment. Social acceptance, which is also known as peer pressure, is the need to be accepted by those whose friendships we value. It's the need to fit in – to look like and act like "our group." It affects children, teenagers and adults. It determines many decisions we make in life – from things like hair style and clothing, to more serious choices such as smoking, drinking, drugs, and joining a gang. But here's the problem. If we seek social acceptance from others, we give them power over us.

"Gang membership is the epitome of the desire for social acceptance, but it's also the ultimate insane behavior. That's because it guarantees a life of incarceration. If we join a gang, we feel accepted, and finally part of a 'family.' But prison is an awfully high price to pay for it.

"Studies show that as we mature, our need for social acceptance decreases, and gang approval seems less important. Most real world gang members are young; that's because by the time they reach 35, they are either locked up for good, or have woken up to the insanity of gang affiliation – and left.

Chapter 7 - Making Friends

"The best way of being socially accepted is by making friends. We would all like to have friends, but it's not easy to make and keep friends.

"A very successful man named Dale Carnegie wrote a book about making friends. He suggested things like smiling when we meet people, and remembering their names. We can become genuinely interested in them by being good listeners and helping them feel important and appreciated. We can learn what they are interested in and encourage them to discuss their interests. We can resist criticism; nothing hurts a friendship more than criticism. And we can minimize talking about ourselves. These are just a few suggestions on making and keeping friends."

Chapter 8 – Cause and Effect

George spoke up, "At the last two meetings you talked about negative self image, and I had the impression that you felt it was responsible for the bad things Al had done. If that's right, how can a negative self image cause us to do bad things?"

"Excellent question," Bill replied. "It's generally agreed that everything we humans do, good or bad, is done for a reason. When Al got locked up this time, he couldn't figure out why he had made such poor choices. Our job here in counseling is to figure out why. Why do we take drugs, why do we break the law, why do we risk being locked up? The good news is that there is always a reason, and if Al can find that reason, then there is a good chance he won't come back here again.

"Our subconscious is the unconscious part of our mind. It's a sector of the brain that holds all the memories of the negative events of our lives going back to our childhood. The conscious part of our brain doesn't remember these many things, but our subconscious does. It also holds the emotions we felt when those hurtful events occurred. If something bad happens to us as adults, we experience negative emotions. If the occurrence is similar to a previous event, our subconscious will bring up our hurt emotions from that experience also. All these painful emotions from both the current and previous events can overwhelm us, and negatively influence our actions today.

"For example, Al felt rejected when the neighbors didn't invite him to go to the beach. Al already had a negative self image which centered on feeling rejected by his mother. The neighbors' 'beach' rejection reinforced his earlier sense of rejection, and overwhelmed him; so he reacted negatively.

"We need to look into our subconscious and find those negative events and emotions from our past. We need to put them in perspective and determine if they are relevant to our lives today. We and only we hold the key to locate all those old events and emotions. If we can find them, then we can deal with them, and we should, because they have the power to drag us back into prison again.

"We humans react in many different ways to negative emotions. Sometimes we cry, sometimes we yell, sometimes we stuff everything inside, and sometimes we get angry and violent. When our emotional pain is overwhelming, we will try anything to end it, including alcohol, drugs or violence.

"Growing up, Al's daily routine was one of abandonment. When he would get home from school, the house would be empty. His mother wouldn't come home until eight at night. He would have to scrounge around for something to eat. When neighbors would be celebrating the holidays, Al was left alone. There was no big dinner at Al's house on Thanksgiving. There was no Christmas tree or presents to be had. Other kids received these things, but Al didn't. He felt abandoned, rejected, left out. All of these difficulties made him feel worthless.

"A feeling of worthlessness causes a certain level of emotional pain. It acts like an open wound. When Al felt rejected by the neighbors and could do nothing about it, he felt helpless. He realized he could do little to fix the situation and felt hopeless. These feelings of helplessness and hopelessness were like knives being poked into his already open wound of worthlessness. His emotional pain was excruciating, and he was ready to do anything to stop that pain.

"Al experienced anger, and he envisioned himself throwing a rock through their window. That thought gave him a rush, which was a relief from his emotional pain. He felt that if he acted on that rush, his emotional pain would go away, and so he threw the rock. And, for a short time, his emotional pain did go away. But then, as time went on, he started feeling guilty.

"So George, your original question was, 'How does having a negative self image cause us to do bad things?' Our negative image makes us feel worthless. If we can do little or nothing about our situation, then we feel helpless and hopeless. We need relief from this emotional pain and feel revenge will provide it. Violence is used as a way of getting that revenge, and for a short time the pain does go away. But eventually we pay for this brief reprieve with the emotion of guilt. And the guilt adds to our worthlessness. The final result is that our negative self image is worse after the violence than before. We counselors have a saying: 'From sad to mad and from mad to bad.' It's what happened to Al."

George asked, "So a feeling of worthlessness is the cause of Al's breaking the window?"

"One of the causes," Bill answered. "If we feel worthless, and find ourselves trapped in a negative situation that we have no control over, we also feel helpless. If we try to improve our situation and have no success, then we feel the situation is hopeless. Psychologists agree that a combination of worthlessness, helplessness and hopelessness are responsible for most suicides. That's because emotional pain can sometimes be even more painful than physical pain.

"But psychologists have also discovered that people suffering from less severe emotional pain will resort to a less severe form of suicide, which is called self destructive behavior (SDB). Al would get angry and break his own toys. That was not in his best interest. It was self destructive behavior – SDB. We'll talk about SDB at a future meeting.

Chapter 9 - A Normal Family

At the next meeting Bill said, "We have been talking about the connection between Al's negative self image and his negative behavior. But I'd like to look at Al's situation from another direction. If Al had been born into a caring environment, where he was shown love and acceptance, he probably would never have felt worthless. Although Al felt worthless, he in fact, was not worthless. His feeling of worthlessness was caused by his environment. Unfortunately, our self image is who we think we are, not who we actually are. If we are repeatedly treated like we are worthless, we will begin to feel we are worthless.

"My contention is that Al's feelings of worthlessness are not Al's fault. Al did nothing wrong to end up with those feelings. His feelings were mostly the result of his mother's neglect and abuse. Also, the hopeless situation he found himself in was not his fault either. Most children have little control over their environment. So, little of Al's negative childhood image was caused by Al himself. It was mostly the result of his mother's negative behavior."

Chapter 10 - Free Will

"So," George asked, "who is responsible for Al's actions – Al or his mother?"

"Al is!" Bill said. "Al is responsible for his own actions. He had the free will to get himself into trouble or not, and he exercised that will in a negative manner. We all have a free will, and we can use it to make any choice we want. Our emotions may be in turmoil caused by others, and we may feel like being destructive. But the decision to act badly is still ours to make. The responsibility for our choice is still on our shoulders.

"I saw a video of a 1 year old who used a chair to climb up on the kitchen table. He crawled across the table to the cookie jar and took the top off. He started to put his hand in the jar, but stopped and looked back to see if anyone was watching.

"We humans know at an early age the difference between right and wrong. Our Creator has given us a free will. If we decide to be destructive to others or ourselves, it is totally our choice. The actions of others may encourage us to lash out, but the choice is always ours, and if we choose poorly, we are probably the ones who will suffer the most!"

Chapter 11 - Support

George spoke up, "Well, if our emotions are in turmoil, then what can we do?"

"That's one of the best questions asked so far," Bill answered, "and the answer is, 'Support!' We need some form of emotional support in our lives, and when we find ourselves in emotional turmoil we run to that support! Right now, this group is a support group. Those of us suffering from self destructive behavior will always need to have support. And we'll need this support as long as we live. That's because we are not immune from the negative events that can cause the emotional turmoil that may drag us back in here.

"Life has its tragedies, and we should expect to experience times of emotional turmoil throughout our lives. There will be accidents, deaths, serious illnesses, relationship failures, and any number of negative incidents which can occur – they are inevitable. If we are not in touch with our feelings, and if we don't have some form of support from others to help us deal with our emotional pain, then we will be unarmed going into battle against our greatest enemy – the enemy within – our self destructive behavior.

"Al's support was his grandfather. When he died, Al had no support person he could run to, no one to counteract his demoralizing situation."

"So," George said, "right now this counseling group is our support."

"Yes," Bill answered, "but counseling groups are just one part of our support. Those who have overcome addiction usually have three or more layers of support available to them. The first layer is our counseling group, which we should attend once a week, or more, the rest of our lives. This could be AA or NA. I think that our loved ones should also go to Al Anon or Narc Anon on a regular basis. They need to be as thoroughly educated as we are about our addiction.

"Also, people who are successful in staying out, often talk about how supportive churches can be. One fellow told me about a church that was dedicated to helping former inmates. He joined it as soon as he got out. They helped him find a job, get an apartment and buy a car. They were a good influence, had positive goals, and were involved in healthy activities. He enrolled his kids in Sunday school, where they made new friends who were dedicated to succeeding in school. He said it was a win, win situation.

"The second layer of support is our sponsor. This is usually someone who has beaten self destructive behavior or addiction, someone whose opinions we respect – usually another NA member.

"Thirdly, those of us who are doing well have a professional counselor or psychologist for support. We can talk to this professional regarding matters that we can't or don't want to bring up with our counseling group or sponsor. Would Al be here today if he had had a sponsor? Probably not.

"All of us will experience emotional pain from time to time. If we have a plan in place, this pain will not drive us to destruction. Here's what we can do when our emotions are in turmoil. First, we can be aware that it's happening. We can recognize our pain and label it. We can say, 'Hey, I'm feeling really bad,' or 'I'm depressed,' or "I'm angry.' Then if we have a sponsor, we can call that person right then, before things get out of hand. We can tell our sponsor what happened and how we are feeling about it. It is critical we get support quickly. If our sponsor is not available, we can talk to someone in our support group who we feel comfortable with.

"If it is a small problem that has been building up for a while, we can probably wait for our NA meeting. But we shouldn't let emotional problems grow. We need to address them as soon as we are aware of them. And, if we have different layers of support, we will always be able to get help when we need it."

George asked, "Can our families be our support if they are going to Narc Anon?"

"Yes," Bill said, "they certainly can. However, our major support should come from outside our family. This is because our most difficult emotional challenges come from disagreements with loved ones. If we have a fight with our wife, we will need an independent third party to talk to about it."

Chapter 12 - Leo's Story

At the next meeting, Leo said, "So far, we've talked about the reasons we've messed up our lives – like negative self image and emotional decisions. I'm supposed to get out soon, so I've been trying to put together a plan to keep me from doing these things in the future."

"That's good," Bill said, "can you tell us your thoughts?"

"Sure," Leo answered. "Let me start by giving some background. I'm an alcoholic, and my drinking has caused me problems with work, family, and friends. One day I was notified they were going to foreclose on my house and car. So I went to my favorite bar and got drunk. On the way home, I crashed into a sign. I got arrested and thrown in jail – it was my third DWI.

"I called my wife to come bail me out. She refused. She told me she was tired of living with my drunkenness and was going to take the kids and go home to her mother. I called my boss and asked him to bail me out, but he also refused. He told me my drinking had caused problems on the job, and now that I had received my third DWI, I was fired.

"A volunteer chaplain came through the jail and saw me sitting on my bunk. He said, 'Hey pal, you look pretty sad. Can I help?' I told him what had happened and described how I had lost everything and that even I was lost. The chaplain said, 'Well you're in luck, because I'm here to seek and save the lost. Have you asked God to help you with your problems?' I told him that I didn't think God would want anything to do with me.

"The chaplain then pulled out a small, pocket New Testament and said, 'Let me show you something.' He opened the book to John 3:16 and started writing on the page. John 3:16 is the passage that says, 'For God so loved the world ...'" Well, everywhere the passage said the word 'world', he scratched it out and replaced it with my name, 'Leo.' He gave me the bible and said, 'Here, read this.' I read the passage, which now said, 'For God so loved <u>Leo</u> that He gave His only Son so that <u>Leo</u> might not perish but have eternal life. For God did not send His Son to judge <u>Leo</u>, but to save him.'

"After I read the passage, I told the chaplain that I wanted to be alone. I found a quiet spot and started thinking about my life and how often I had disappointed my family and myself. I thought about the people I had hurt, and all the times I had been hurt.

"I thought about all the good opportunities that had been presented to me, and how I had failed at almost every one. Then I thought about my wife and kids, and how much love they had shown me, and how seldom I had responded to it.

"I opened the bible and read the passage again, 'For God so loved Leo . . .,' then closed it and started to cry. I cried for my kids, for my wife, for my parents, for all those I loved and had disappointed. Then I cried for myself.

"When I woke up the next day I decided to read about this God who loved me in spite of my failures. So I started reading the bible and studying this God of love. The chaplain brought me a bible study guide and other study materials to help me learn about God's forgiveness. And he also brought me books on alcoholism.

"So I've been studying these things like crazy, and when we talked about negative self image, I realized I have one, too. But mine wasn't so much caused by a bad childhood, as by my own drunken behavior. I can't blame anyone else for my bad self image. I alone am to blame."

"That's a good observation," Bill remarked. "Do I get the impression that you feel better now?"

"Yes," Leo said. "I feel much better. And I'm working on forgiveness. I've been telling all those I've hurt how bad I feel about hurting them, and I've been asking them to forgive me. I have the feeling that God has forgiven me, and I've made great progress in forgiving myself. And all this is helping me feel much better about myself."

"That shows progress," Bill said. "Your work on forgiveness has helped you remove much of the guilt you have been carrying around. It has helped you remove many of the negative emotions that have been diminishing your self image, and it is making you feel better about yourself. This is an important step toward success in staying out. Have you put together a plan to stay out?"

"Yes," Leo said. "Do you want to hear it?"

"Of course," Bill said.

Chapter 13 - Leo's Plan

"**First**," Leo said, "I'm going to join a church. All my life I've been hanging around with other drinkers like myself. I need new friends.

"**Second**, I'm going to go to AA. I'm going to do 90 meetings in 90 days. That's what they recommend.

"**Third**, I'm going to try to get my job back. I wrote to my boss and his letter back to me was encouraging.

"**Fourth**, after I've been out for a month, and still sober, I'm going to visit my wife and see if she will forgive me and consider getting back together. We've also been writing.

"**Fifth**, if my wife accepts me back, I'm going to try to get her and the kids into counseling of some kind. Maybe the church will have something, or maybe they can go to Al Anon.

"**Sixth**, if I get my job back, I'm going to start an AA program at work for the other employees who have problems with drinking."

"Well," Bill said, "that sounds like a good plan. You said you were going to be released soon. Please write and tell us how well your plan works."

Chapter 14 – Emotions

At the next meeting, Bill asked, "Does anyone have any questions or issues they want to discuss?"

Al said, "I've been telling the fellows back in the pod about some of the things we've talked about here. They asked me if I would help them start an NA group of their own in the pod. I asked them how many wanted to attend, and five men said they did. Is that OK? How would we do it?

"Well," Bill said, "it's very good that the men want to start their own group. But it's important to have a moderator who would know what subjects to cover and to help keep everyone focused on the day's topic. Who would be your moderator?"

"Well," Al said, "they asked me if I would lead the group because I have been participating here and know what goes on."

"I think you'd be good," Bill said, "and I encourage you to do it. You might want to discuss topics such as negative self image, self destructive behavior, emotions, and guilt. I encourage you to go ahead and start. I'll try to get you an NA leader's guide."

George spoke up, "In a previous meeting, you talked about people committing suicide. Do many people commit suicide who come to NA?"

"Actually," Bill answered, "once people start attending regularly, the potential for suicide decreases to almost zero. As I mentioned before, most suicides are caused by our emotions – severe emotional pain. In NA we work on our emotions and try to identify issues that might trigger negative emotions. When we examine our emotions, we start seeing them from a rational point of view. This can decrease their severity, and we can see them for what they are, just emotions. They are not who we are, but only how we are feeling at that moment.

"When we can define our emotions, and describe them with a word, like anxious, jealous, depressed, or angry, then it helps us to look at them from the outside. It's like holding them up to the light and examining them. If our emotions are painful, and if we can label them, then they lose their intensity. I think that's because we are looking at them in a more objective way; we are seeing them as they really are – just feelings. When we can see them as they really are, then they don't define who we really are, and they lose much of their control over us."

George asked, "How do emotions control us?"

"Good question," Bill responded. "There is a saying that intellect makes the best decisions, and emotions can make the worst. We need to be able to differentiate between intellectual thoughts and emotional impulses. If we look at the decisions that caused our incarceration, we will probably see that they were driven by our emotions.

"Al's road to his present incarceration began when he started back on cocaine. He remembered many negative things from his old life, and they were causing him deep emotional pain. His habit had been to medicate that pain with drugs. In other words, his emotions were driving him to take drugs. He shouted to himself, 'What's wrong with me?' That was his intellect trying to tell him this action was wrong. His intellect was attempting to counteract his emotions. But he hadn't learned to examine or control his emotions. He didn't understand why he was feeling depressed. His emotions were not under the control of his intellect, so he made a poor emotional decision.

"In counseling, the reason we spend so much time dealing with our emotions is so we can keep them under control; we don't want them to make our decisions for us; we want our intellect to make our decisions.

"And when I say, 'keep them under control,' I don't mean, 'stuff them inside.' On the contrary, we need to bring them out in the open – to talk to someone about them – preferably our sponsor. That helps keep them under control."

George asked, "can you explain that a little further?"

"Sure," Bill said, "If we want to stay on top of our emotions, we need to do five things. **First,** recognize our current emotions. **Second,** name them. **Third,** determine the cause. **Fourth,** ask, 'Are these emotions encouraging action?' And **Fifth,** ask, 'Is that action good for me?'

"Let me give you an example. A fellow named Fred, who has been attending my 'free world' NA group for 18 years, told me a story. He was in line at the grocery store, his line was moving very slowly, and the other lines were going faster. His mind started telling him that this was not worth waiting for, and that he should leave the store.

"Fred has been working on his emotions for a long time, and that thought helped him recognize that his emotions were running high. He came to get food for that day's meals and it would be illogical to leave because he'd eventually have to drive all the way back and pick out groceries again.

"So the first step in taking control of his emotions was recognizing that they were running high. And he did. He said to himself, 'What's going on here? Why do I feel like doing something illogical? These are my emotions talking. I need to stop for a moment and think this through. What am I feeling? I'm feeling frustrated. Naming this is good; I've identified the emotion – frustration.'

"Next, can I figure out why I'm frustrated? The other lines are moving, but a credit card problem has stopped my line, so I'm frustrated. Good, I've determined why my emotions are high. Are they encouraging me to take action? Yes, my frustrated emotions want me to leave the store – how illogical – but emotions usually are illogical.

"So, now I need to make my intellect override my emotions. Am I in a hurry? No, I have plenty of time to get this shopping done, and this credit card problem will probably be resolved shortly. I also have the option of moving to another line. So, I need to calm down, close my eyes and feel peace.

"This was a good test of controlling my emotions. I recognized they are running high, I've identified them, I've found their cause and I know what actions they are trying to get me to take. Most importantly, my intellect is taking control instead of my emotions.'

"Fred's story is just one small example of how to recognize emotions and deal with them logically. But he is an addict in control of his disease for 18 years, so he knows he has to monitor his emotions continuously.

"But staying on top of our emotions only comes with practice and experience. We have to stay in touch with them at all times. Fred does this by talking to himself throughout the day, and it's changed his life. His emotions don't rule him anymore. If we can understand our emotions, and if we can control our decisions, then our self destructive behavior won't rise up to bite us."

"So," George asked, "talking to ourselves about our emotions all day long is how we get control of them?"

"Yes," Bill said, "That's exactly right. We need to talk to ourselves throughout the day about our emotions. We need to get in the habit of asking ourselves how we're feeling all the time. It's OK to talk to ourselves, it's very healthy.

"Also very important to this process is keeping an emotional journal. At the end of each day, the fellows who've overcome addiction write down the emotions they've experienced during the day. And they go back and review different days and compare them. They've told me that it's one of the best tools they have in battling addiction. Rarely do their emotions make decisions for them anymore. I realize this seems like a lot of work to begin with, but if we stick with it, it becomes a good habit.

"And speaking of good habits, it's important to get in a good routine; to get up, go to work and eat meals on schedule each day. It's good to go to support each week and meet our sponsor regularly. Getting in a good routine keeps life organized, consistent and predictable. A good routine helps keep stress to a minimum, and our emotions under control. That way the unexpected won't degrade our emotions."

Chapter 15 - Unseen Scars

George said, "We've been talking about emotions, and it's got me thinking. When I was in foster, I got in a lot of fights – one of which got me four stitches in my head. My foster dad brought me home and examined my wound. He said it was within my hairline and when my hair grew out it would be unseen – nothing to worry about.

"But then he told me I had other deeper unseen scars – scars on my heart from being taken away from my mother, and scars from the way my step father treated me. And I understood what he was talking about. And the concept of scars on my heart has helped me to understand what we've been talking about here when we talk about our emotions and especially about our negative self image.

"But it's tough to re-examine those unseen scars, because it's like opening up old wounds. And when I open them up again, the pain is still there, like when I got them the first time – and that's too much pain. I'd rather not do it. I'd rather they remain unseen – out of mind."

"They may be unseen to our conscious mind," Bill said. "But our subconscious mind won't let us forget them. So unless we deal with them, they will just continue to resurface again and again to infect our emotions and encourage us to self destruct. So if we want to stay out of prison we need to deal with these emotional gremlins from our past, no matter how painful it is to do so."

Chapter 16 - Self Destructive Behavior

At the next meeting Bill said, "I have some good news. Leo has been paroled and has gone home. He said he would write us as soon as he got settled. Does anyone have any thoughts?"

"Yes," Juan said. "I like that kind of news. It gives us hope we will all get to leave here one day.

"I agree," Al said. "And you know, I don't know why, but coming here is giving me hope. Since telling the group about my lousy childhood and all the bad things I've done, I'm starting to feel a lot better inside. I'm feeling a sense of hope and peace. I don't think I've ever felt real peace before. When I first started here, I didn't see the point of talking about my feelings. But since I've been exploring my past, I'm starting to understand it and put it behind me – and I'm starting to feel better about myself."

"Well," Bill said, "That's a great way to start the meeting. Does anyone have any questions?"

George said, "In reviewing my notes, I've found the term self destructive behavior. What exactly is that?"

"I'm glad you asked," Bill replied, "because it's one of the main reasons we get involved in crime.

"Most people who find themselves locked up have a condition that psychologists call, self-destructive behavior, or SDB for short. This destructive behavior has many forms – from serious behavior like alcohol, drug abuse or criminality, to lesser forms like smoking and overeating. SDB could be as simple as ignoring a disease like diabetes or high cholesterol, or something more serious like self mutilation or drunken driving. Compulsive gambling and delinquency are forms of SDB. Most people who are locked up suffer from some form of SDB.

"Many people who have been diagnosed with SDB by a psychologist also suffer from low self esteem and depression – which most professionals feel are contributors to SDB.

"In addition, many people have an overwhelming need for social acceptance, and they fulfill that need with gang affiliation – a form of SDB which usually leads to incarceration.

"Al's decision to get involved in a drive by shooting is an example of self destructive behavior. He received a week's worth of drugs; it cost him four years in prison. But Al's real self destruction was taking the cocaine in the first place. He knew it was wrong to do, as is clearly shown in his cry of 'What's wrong with me?' He knew there would be serious consequences, yet he did it anyway. That's a classic case of self destructive behavior.

"Hurting ourselves is not normal behavior. It's not logical to cause our own destruction, it borders on insanity. But there is usually a valid reason for our SDB, so if we can find the reason, then we can remove it. Finding and removing our SDB is the key to staying out of prison.

"Has anyone else had a problem with self destructive behavior?"

Chapter 17 - Donardo's Story

Donardo spoke up, "I came close to killing myself with my car. I'm in here for reckless driving. I had a fight with my wife, and it was a bad one. So I got in my car and started driving like a crazy man. I ran a red light at the corner of our street and ran another as I got on the expressway. For the next half hour, I drove the car as fast as it would go. I weaved in and out of traffic and laid on my horn at anyone who wouldn't get out of my way. I came close to hitting one guy from behind.

"The police started chasing me and boxed me in. I ran off the road and was heading for a large tree, but I swerved and ended up in some bushes. I was arrested, and now I'm here."

"So," Bill said, "it all started with a fight with your wife. Can you go back and describe what you were feeling at the time?"

"I was angry," Donardo said. "I don't remember ever being that angry before. All I can remember is anger."

"Well," Bill said, "your actions are a good example of emotions making bad decisions. Of course, you could have killed yourself. Did that occur to you?"

"Actually," Donardo said, "I didn't much care whether I lived or died. I just needed to do something – take some action. I kind of remember thinking, 'I'll kill myself, and that will teach her.' "

"Yes," Bill said, "that is definitely a self destructive thought – not caring if you killed yourself. Do you still feel that way?"

"No, no," Donardo said, "I was over my anger in a little while. And then I was really disappointed in myself for doing such a stupid thing – letting my anger get so far out of control."

"Alright," Bill said, "let's examine this for a minute. Sometimes we use SDB as a way of coping. You felt anger and needed to do something about it. Your emotions were painful and out of control, and you chose to cope with them by driving crazy. At some level you might have been saying to yourself, 'maybe the pain will go away if I do something shocking. It will take my mind off the pain.' But you also had the thought that if you killed yourself, it would teach your wife a lesson. Can you go into that a little more?"

"I wanted to get back at her for fighting with me. I was angry and wanted to hurt her."

"Yes," Bill said, "if she loves you, and you hurt yourself, it hurts her. You were using SDB as a form of revenge. Or, if you hurt yourself she might feel sorry for you and not be mad at you anymore. You were using SDB to get her sympathy. Or you might have been seeking attention. Maybe you were saying, 'Don't you see how hurt and upset you have made me?' When someone loves us, we can use SDB to manipulate them simply because the people who love us the most are the ones we can hurt the most. But also, the people we love the most are the ones who can hurt us the most. If someone we love says something negative to us, it hurts much more than if a stranger said the same thing. My guess is that during the fight, you probably said ugly things to each other."

"Yes," Donardo said, "I remember her calling me stupid. I always felt stupid in school because I have a learning disability called dyslexia and was held back twice. My parents never praised me; they were always on my case because of my poor grades. I was the dummy. So her calling me stupid really hurt, because it reminded me of my childhood feelings. But I probably hurt her also with the names I called her."

"Yes," Bill said, "and that may have caused you to feel guilty about what you said to her. Also, the fight may have been so hurtful that you may have felt she didn't love you anymore. That might add fear to the hurt and guilt you were feeling. So you bundled all these intense emotions up into one out-of-control emotion – anger. Psychologists describe this as, 'sad to mad and mad to bad.' "

"Yes," Donardo said, "I think that getting back at her by hurting myself, was my way of telling her that I was really hurt. It was the best way I could show her how angry I was. I guess I'm kind of crazy."

"If you're crazy," Bill said, "then we're all crazy, because all humans, from judges to janitors, have SDB to some degree.

"It's also common for kids to use SDB to get attention. If they are upset with some part of their lives, kids will purposely fail in school or get in trouble because they want to have some input into their negative situation. Misbehavior is a way of getting their parents' attention. Once they have it, they can voice their displeasure. This gives them some control in their lives, even if they have to pay for it by being punished for their misbehavior.

"But the bottom line is that your SDB of reckless driving was caused by out of control emotions. It is a good example of why we need to keep our emotions under control."

Chapter 18 - SDB as Revenge

"You mentioned," Donardo said, "that sometimes SDB is used as a form of revenge. Could you give me an example?"

"Yes I can," Bill said. "Many years ago I was doing counseling work with a chaplain, and as we entered a gang pod, a security officer was yelling at one of the inmates for being a trouble maker. The inmate yelled at the officer, 'Do you know who I am?' The officer shot back, 'You're a piece of s***!'

"I'll never forget the look on the inmate's face when he heard it – he looked like he'd been stabbed with a knife. The chaplain also saw his hurt and took him aside and said, 'No, no – he's wrong – you're not a piece of s***. God created you, and God doesn't make junk. The hurt on your face told me someone has called you that before – maybe it was when you were a little boy and you were hoping someone would understand what you were going through, but instead you were called a piece of s***. Whoever told you that was wrong. God loves you more than you will ever know. Ignore anyone telling you any differently.

"A few weeks later the chaplain told me that he received a note from that inmate asking if they could meet. They met and the inmate told him that his mother's boyfriend used to call him a piece of s*** all the time. When he would hear those words he would say to himself 'Oh yeah, you think I'm s***? Well I'll show you how much of a piece of s*** I can really be.' And then he would go out and purposely get in as much trouble he could as a way of getting back at the boyfriend.

"But the story has a happy ending, because the inmate realized that the only person he was really hurting was himself, and that was crazy, especially since his mother had sent the boyfriend packing years before. However, using SDB as a form of revenge is not uncommon."

Chapter 19 - The Uniqueness of Our Lives

"You know," Bill said, "we've spent most of our time exploring the negative areas of our past. So I'd like to read you something positive that I received from Sam Medrano. He was in this group about a year ago. He's out now and doing well. Here's what he wrote: 'There is only one of us in the universe; and we each have unique assets and liabilities. Do we define ourselves by our talents – or by our limitations? Do we see the greatness in our gifts or the futility in our faults? Do we applaud our assets or flounder in our failures? Do we see the potential of our possibilities or the extent of our errors?

We are only given one life. To live this life fully we need to accept ourselves for who we are, and stop worrying about who we are not. We can see ourselves in what we can do, not what we haven't done. It's foolish to measure ourselves against the accomplishments of others. It's better to measure ourselves by how we use our talents. Our easiest success is offering ourselves in service to others. In this way we feel worth.

It's no crime to fall down – everyone does that. The crime is in not getting up or not helping up others who have fallen. Are we working to become the heroes of our lives?

Chapter 20 – Juan's Story

At the next meeting Juan said, "I've been taking notes, and reviewing them after each meeting. I think I now understand self image. It's how we view ourselves. Negative self image is caused by bad things happening to us, or people saying bad things about us when we were at a very vulnerable age. Or it's feeling guilty for the bad things we've done; we feel we don't measure up. But I was wondering, is it possible to change our negative image to a positive one?"

"Great question," Bill replied, "The answer is yes! There are many things that can be done to turn a negative self image into a positive one. And improving our image should be one of our top priorities. Could you give us some background on your life?"

"Well," Juan said, "It's not pretty. My mother died giving birth to me. My father was an alcoholic. He and my two older brothers blamed me for her death, and they made my life a living hell. I have memories of my father choking and cursing me. Frequently, he would hit me on the side of my head with the back of his hand as he'd walk by me. Many times he came home drunk and would start beating me with the buckle end of his belt, accusing me of causing my mother's death. I found the emotional pain of this accusation to be even worse than the physical pain of the beating.

"My brothers would often lock me in a closet for hours, sometimes overnight, leaving me without food or water. I was their whipping boy, their stone throwing target, or their punching bag. But the worst part was the hurtful names they'd call me. They treated me like dirt.

"I think I was 7 when I started staying away from home as much as possible. When I was 12 my father came home very drunk and started in on me with his belt. I ran out of that house and never went back. I lived under the bleachers of the football stadium. On the days I went to school I could get the free breakfast and lunch. Sometimes I would wash dishes at a restaurant nearby, and they would let me have all the leftovers. On cold nights, I would head to the homeless shelter. They provided me with meals and used clothing.

"There were some fellows from school I would hang with. We started stealing beer and wine from the 7-11, and I think I was 15 when we started smoking grass. It wasn't long before we were selling it to the other kids at school. That put us in Juvie, but I didn't care. Anything was better than home.

"After my time in Juvie, I went to a foster home. The folks there weren't too bad, but I was used to being on my own, so I left. But they found me and put me at Hope House for boys. I left there too, and was in and out of foster care until I got busted at 17 with 5 pounds of grass. I got two years at TDCJ for that offense."

"You said you ate meals at school." Bill said. "Did you attend classes?"

"Yeah," Juan said, "I had nothing else to do, and my friends were there. I was a senior when I got busted, so I didn't graduate."

"So," Bill said, "did you decide to change your life in TDCJ?"

"No," Juan said. "I joined a gang there and stayed with it after I got out. They were like family to me. We worked out of a stash house, sold drugs, boosted cars, that sort of thing. I moved in with one of the girls in our gang. We experimented with every drug and pill we could find. We'd work for the gang a couple hours a day selling drugs, and then stay high the rest of the time.

"It was a life without pain. But my mind started getting weird. I had tons of drugs, anything I wanted, and plenty of money. But the more drugs I took, the worse my thinking got. I started imagining that my gang was out to get me. I got a gun, two guns, three guns – but it wasn't enough. The drugs had made me paranoid – suspicious of everyone. I was ready to shoot anyone who came near our home.

"My girl told me I had lost my mind and left me. So, I started trying other drugs, hoping it would help me feel better. Funny, I had everything I wanted – drugs, money, car, a house – and yet, life inside my head was pure hell.

"One day as I was leaving the house, three police cars surrounded me and took me down. Now this may sound crazy, but as they were putting the cuffs on me, I felt an unbelievable relief – like I was finally safe.

"I spent 8 days of hell in detox. When I was finally sane and thinking clearly, I realized that my gang wasn't out to get me after all. I had imagined the whole thing. The drugs had made me crazy. Anyway, now I'm doing 5 years and trying to decide what to do with my life."

Chapter 21 - Changing Our Self Image

"Well," Bill said, "That's quite a story; and when we have a lot of bad things like that happen to us in our youth, it usually damages our image. So it's in our best interest to improve that image. Here's how we can do that. "**First**, it is very helpful to write down the things that have hurt our image; the negative things that have happened to us, and the hurtful things people have said about us – those we can remember. This should help identify the negative side of our image."

"So," Juan said, "would that be things like my father and brothers telling me it was my fault my mother died giving birth to me?"

"Exactly," Bill said. "That's a perfect example. You've identified something that hurt your image – they told you 'it was your fault your mother died.' Now, once you've identified it, then the **Second** thing we can do is to determine where that negative idea came from. And you've done that, too; it came from your family. So you have identified the negative image and determined where it came from.

"Now the **Third** thing is to decide if this image is true or not."

"My uncle told me I wasn't at fault," Juan said. "He said that if anyone was at fault it was my father because he was passed out drunk when it came time to drive my mom to the hospital. Others have told me the same thing."

"Of course it wasn't your fault," Bill said, "and you realize that. So if what we were told wasn't true, then the **Fourth** thing we can do is to start removing those words from our mind. And when we do, our self image will start to improve. Even just realizing that an idea wasn't true starts to remove it from our mind."

"So," Juan said, "I need to write all this down – that 'I was told it was my fault my mother died, that my father and brothers told me this, that my uncle and others told me it wasn't true and that it is time for me to put it out of my mind – to change the way I think about myself. I can feel good about myself when I think about my mother.'"

"Right," Bill said. "But also, you can make an affirmation – you can tell yourself something positive. Since our current poor image is the result of hurtful things told to us as children, we can replace those hurtful words with positive words. If we were told we were stupid as a child, we can look at all the intelligent things we have done in our lives and then tell ourselves, or affirm to ourselves, that we are in fact smart, not stupid."

"So," Juan said, "I can say that I was told it was my fault that my mom died, but in fact that is not true, that my mom died because she wasn't given proper medical care at childbirth. And if she had lived she would have loved me very much."

"Excellent," Bill said. "And besides saying good things, we can do good things. Helping others is very healthy for our self image. We can listen to someone if they need to talk. We can share what we have. We can help someone with his chores.

"Another thing," Juan said, "Was it bad when I ran away from home?"

"No," Bill said. "It wasn't bad, it was survival. You were repeatedly abused, and you defended yourself by running away; it's how you dealt with your situation. However foster wasn't bad, but still you reacted to it in the same way you reacted to your home situation. You see, there is a difference between a reaction and a well thought through decision. A reaction is more like a habit. Perhaps if you had given foster a chance, and learned to follow the rules there, you wouldn't be here today."

"I hadn't thought about that before," Juan said. "I didn't really give foster a chance."

"Right," Bill said. "However, you were in the habit of reacting to situations back then rather than sitting down and making logical decisions. Today however, you are an adult, and you can make logical decisions when you run into problems rather than reacting to them. That is something we all need to think about when facing problems – do we react – or do we decide? Do we react to situations in the same way we did as children, or do we think through the situations we encounter and make logical adult decisions?

"OK, a **Fifth** way we improve our image is to take our list of things that hurt our image and next to each one we can write down how we would like ourselves to be. We can call this our **Wish List**. For example, in my wish list I wrote, 'when I'm on drugs, I lie like hell to everyone.' Then after that I wrote, 'I can change. I can improve my behavior and I won't have to lie.' "

"So," Juan said, "next to the item on my list that I sold drugs, I can say, 'I'm not going to use or sell drugs in the future.' "

"Yes," Bill said, "that's a good example. Then when we finish adding in all the ways we would like to be, we can go down the list and determine if it's possible to make these changes. If we think we can, then we can imagine what our self image would look like with these 'wish list' changes. We might find ourselves saying, 'Wow, I can see myself as a really good person!'

"Putting things in black and white and reviewing them regularly will greatly help to improve our self image.

"**Sixth**, we can help others; we can have an outreach. At some level, we all want to be heroes, and when we help those in need we become heroes, and that gives us a feeling of worth. Besides being heroes, helping others can be a way of making amends or payback for the negative things we have done.

"**Seventh**, if we have ever hurt anyone, we can ask them for forgiveness. Asking for forgiveness improves our self image and our sense of peace – especially if we hurt someone we really care for.

"**Eighth**, we can try to love others. Think about this, love isn't love unless we give it away. And, the more love we give, the more love we have. Love is very positive for our self image.

"**Ninth**, there are things we can do each day to lift our spirits and improve our image. We can write down our good traits and review them each morning, including how we intend to act in the future; we can write down positive things that happen to us each day; we can show gratitude to those who have helped us; we can set a goal and work a little each day to achieve it; we can recall good memories as we go to bed each night. All of these things are beneficial to our self image.

"But, there is also another side to a negative image. It's possible to use a negative self-image to justify our failures. 'I'll never be any good, so why should I try?' 'I'll never succeed at anything.' Are we using our self image as an excuse to fail?

"For every person who is afraid of failure, there is at least one other who is afraid of success. And if we succeed, we may be expected to continue succeeding. That may require too much effort or put us under too much pressure – and so we fail.

"Do we want to succeed in staying out? If so, a positive self image is important; and there are many things we can do to improve it.

Chapter 22 - Subconscious Juvenile Instructions

The meeting opened and Bill said, "At the last meeting Juan told us his story. His childhood years are an excellent example of subconscious juvenile instructions. As children, we react to difficult situations in childish ways. Then as adults, when we experience similar situations, we tend to react to them in the same way we did as kids. We call this decision making system, subconscious juvenile instructions, and we make our decisions based on these childish instructions, rather than using mature rational thinking.

"For example, when Juan was little, his father and brothers were in charge of him, they treated him terribly, and he ran away. In Juvie and foster he was also under someone's control. These places were not bad, but since they were controlling him, they reminded him of home, and he ran from them too. He was following subconscious instructions from his earlier years. He had learned that when he was under control of others, he got hurt, and it was best to run away, and so he did.

"When he joined a gang, they had rules and control, so he ran from them and lived apart with his girl – just as he had done at home, Juvie and foster. He was simply following the subconscious instructions from his youth, which told him to run from controlling situations. Although he thought he was running from control, he was in fact, being controlled by the distressed 12 year old he used to be.

"It's quite common for adults to get in the habit of listening to subconscious juvenile instructions. But if our childhoods were traumatic, we have to realize that we cannot trust our gut reactions, and we need to consider a complete rebuilding of our decision making system."

Chapter 23 - Juan's Image

Juan said, "At the last meeting we talked about making a list of negative images and next to those images we can put affirmations or wishes of the way we would like to be. Shall I read mine?"

"Please do," Bill said.

Juan's Wish List

Negative: My father and brothers told me it was my fault my mother died giving birth to me.
Positive Affirmation: My uncle and others told me it was not my fault. Babies have no control.
N: My father beat me. I had 2 older brothers who treated me terribly. They made me feel like dirt.

P: I don't have to go back home. I am trying to forgive my father and brothers.

N: I was in the juvenile habit of running away from home and foster care. I lived on the street. I never graduated from high school.

P: I can use adult logic to make my decisions now. I can find a job and a home. I have my GED.

N: I am ashamed and guilty for going to jail and prison. I'm worried I'll come back again.

P: After detox I felt alive. I'm in counseling. I can create a plan to stay out, and follow that plan.

N: I hung with the wrong people. I joined a gang.

P: That was my need for social acceptance. I have good people in my life today. I know who is helping me to do right and who is not.

N: I got hooked on drugs.

P: I love being sober. I've worked hard at NA and have learned a lot. I will line up strong support.

N: I sold drugs and committed many crimes.

P: I asked God for forgiveness and He has forgiven me. I went to jail and paid my debt to society.

N: I felt I had no skills.

P: I am smart. God already has plans for me! I'm good with tools and my hands.

"That's what I have so far," Juan said, "What do you think?"

"Very good," Bill said. "I think you have a good handle on defeating the negatives in your past."

Chapter 24 – Juan's Plan

When the meeting started, Juan said, "I've been trying to put together a written plan that I can follow when I get out. The first thing in my plan is changing the direction of my life. When Al got out he changed his friends, he got a good job, and he joined sports teams. But he didn't change his thinking, his emotions or his self image, and that caused his problems. So, that means we need to change our friends, job, thinking, emotions, self image and maybe even some of our family."

That's right," said Bill.

"But I also wrote that we need support," Juan said.

"Yes," Bill said. "We need that too. We need a place to run to when we are distressed and are thinking of taking drugs. We need NA or AA, a Church, a sponsor, or a professional counselor. It would be nice to have all of these."

"Yes," Juan said, "And the last topic in my notes is self destructive behavior. So I need to organize all these things into a plan, but I'm not sure where to start. How can I design my plan to cover all this stuff?"

"A written plan is an excellent idea," Bill said, "So far you've talked about long term and short term goals; that's a good start. But we also have tasks that we need to complete each day. If you can put both goals and tasks in your plan, you will have a formula for success.

"Our main goal is to change our lives – to go from the way we were to the way we want to be. To do this, we need to decide what we want to do about a job, a place to live, a vehicle, and our family situation. We need to find multiple levels of support. On a daily basis we can stay in touch with our emotions, and work to enhance our self image."

"So," Juan said, "I'll start with, 'goals,' and under that I'll put, 'My main goal is to completely change my life.'

Then under that I'll list the things I need to address: 'friends, job, home, vehicle, family, support, emotions, self image and SDB.' Under the subject 'New Friends' I think I'll write, 'Find a Church.' I really like the idea of joining a church and making new friends. All my old friends are into the drug life, and I want to get away from that. As far as job goes, I've spent a little of time in construction. Even though I didn't get very good at any particular skill, I did enjoy being a trim carpenter and building cabinets. I think if I put my mind to it, I could become a really good cabinet maker. So under the subject, 'A Job,' I'm going to write, 'Become a Skilled Carpenter."

"You're doing well," Bill said.

"Now under home," Juan said, "I'm going to put, 'New Apartment and Neighborhood.' I don't want to go back to my old neighborhood – too many temptations – I want to start fresh. Then under A Vehicle, I'm going to put down, 'Old Chevy.' My uncle has an old Chevy that needs a lot of work. He told me if I fixed it up I could have it. Next, under My Family, I'm going to write, 'Join a Church.' Maybe the church people can find me a better place to live. Then under 'Find Support,' I'm going to put four items, 'Church, NA, Sponsor and Pastor.' I'm hoping I can find a sponsor in NA, and some churches have pastors that are professional counselors. But, I'm not sure what to put under emotions, negative self image or SDB categories. What do I do about those?"

"That's a good question," Bill said, "because dealing with our emotions is not like finding a job. We have to come to terms with our emotions every day. To that end, one of the things we can do is to review our emotions at the end of the day, and write them down in a journal."

"So," Juan said, "under the subject, 'Acknowledge Emotions,' I'm going to write, 'Emotional Journal.' What else can I put?"

Chapter 25 – Mantra

"Well," Bill said, "you may want to have a mantra – something that you tell yourself throughout the day, in order to stay positive. That's what I do. At the beginning of the day, or before I go out the door, I remind myself to, 'Love everyone, accept everything, enjoy every moment.' This helps put me in a positive mood as I face the challenges and stresses of the day.

"If I'm not careful, I get easily frustrated by the little inconveniences of life, so I need something to keep me focused. For instance, I might leave for work and come up behind a slow driver, become irritated and start thinking, 'Why did this person have to be here at this moment.'

"If, on the other hand, I'm thinking, 'love everyone,' then when I encounter the slow driver, I think positively of him. If I'm thinking, 'accept everything,' then I'll realize that slow drivers are encountered once in a while, and since I've left early enough for work, this is not a big issue. If I'm thinking, 'enjoy every moment,' then I'll relax, breathe out, and thank God that He has given me a moment to enjoy. If I can do this, the little frustrations of life don't affect me as much.

"Sometimes I'll find myself frustrated and angry over something small, and realize that I don't want to be in this negative mood. I'll stop whatever I'm doing and repeat to myself, 'love everyone, accept everything, enjoy every moment,' and my mood will quickly change for the better. If we try to live by our mantra and say it every day and throughout the day, we will find our overall level of happiness increasing as each day goes by; at least that's been my experience."

"That sounds like a good suggestion," Juan said. "I'll put that in my plan. So under the subject 'Acknowledge Emotions,' I'll have the items, 'Emotional Journal' and 'Mantra.' What else?"

"OK," Bill said, "one of the most important factors in all of this is the ability to deal with intense emotional negativity – like a relationship break up, or anger, or despair. Previously, we discussed the five steps to dealing with extreme emotions. **First**, recognize they are running high. **Second**, name them. **Third**, determine their cause. **Fourth**, ask, 'Are these emotions encouraging some kind of action?' And **Fifth**, ask, 'Is that action good for me?'

"Basically, we want to switch from emotional decision making to intellectual decision making. We want to discourage ourselves from making poor decisions while our emotions are running high. Also, we can remember to seek out our sponsor. But most importantly, we can't allow these high emotions to talk us into medicating them with drugs. All this should be in our plan."

"Great idea," Juan commented. "I think I'll add a third item under the subject, 'Acknowledge Emotions.' I'm going to call it, 'Emotions Running High.' Under that item, I can list those five steps to dealing with high emotions, followed by, 'Call Sponsor,' 'No Decisions,' and 'No Drugs.' How does that sound?"

"Sounds good," said Bill, "anything else?"

"Yes," Juan said, "I've put some more items on my affirmation list. They are, 'God created us and God doesn't make junk,' 'I'm God's valued creation' and 'I can be the hero of my life.' I think those should be helpful. But I still need a plan for my self destructive behavior."

Ch 26 - Self Destructive Behavior (SDB) II

"Ok," Bill said, "we covered SDB before, but it is critical for us to understand why we try to hurt ourselves. If we can find the reason for our self destruction, it will be the key to never coming back here again.

"SDB is a progression of harmful or abusive actions toward ourselves. Self destructive actions may be deliberate, born of impulse, or developed as a habit. These actions can be addicting, and are, thus, potentially fatal. All SDB has causes and, thankfully, all SDB can be controlled. So, if we can find the cause, we can create a plan to control it.

"SDB may be used as a way of coping with a particular situation. For example, a man may be out of work and under pressure from his family to get a job. If he feels he can't get one, he may get himself injured, or fall ill, or get arrested. Then he has an excuse to not look for work, and the pressure goes away.

"Or, a man loves a woman, but drives her away because he has a negative self image and thinks he is not good enough for her. Oftentimes a successful person will sabotage his/her own achievements because of a feeling of unworthiness. Al did this. He was doing well in his job and in sports but felt guilty that he didn't deserve this success, so he took drugs to medicate his guilt.

"SDB may be a form of self-punishment in response to a personal failure, or a disappointment or anger. Donardo did this when he went on his driving rampage. He was angry with himself and his wife for the fight they had.

"SDB can easily spiral out of control through alcoholism and drug abuse, which may have resulted from a negative self image. A person drinks or takes drugs to medicate the pain of their poor self opinion, but this may lead to bad behavior or poor job performance or relationship issues – resulting in a downward spiral of drug abuse, negative actions, negative image, more drug abuse, more negative actions, etc. This describes both Al and Juan.

"Joining a gang is a form of SDB. We might have a strong need for social acceptance, but have felt rejected and unwanted in the past. So we join a gang even though it will probably cause our incarceration. Juan had been rejected by his family, so he joined a neighborhood gang in his teens and a professional gang in prison.

"Most kids react to their negative image by seeking attention through SDB as the class clown or by becoming disruptive or destructive. This is what Al did. Many times their poor image is caused by the trauma of poor school performance due to a learning disability and the resulting feeling of 'stupidity' because they can't keep up with their classmates. Or their poor image may be caused by parental abandonment or neglect, or physical, verbal or sexual abuse. This describes Al, Juan and George who all had very difficult childhoods.

"So, SDB is our response to any negative aspects of our lives. We may realize even before we take the action that the consequences will be harmful to us, but we take the action anyway. Our job is to discover the negative aspects that are pushing us to self destruct. Once we discover what they are, we can put together a plan to keep our SDB under control for the rest of our lives."

Chapter 27 - Controlling Our SDB

"So," Juan said, "what do we put in our plan to control our SDB?"

"We all have SDB to some degree," Bill said, "and our SDB has many causes. Before writing our plan we have to identify those causes. We might have a negative self image, ongoing guilt, fear of success, a habit of failure or an addiction to drugs or alcohol. We need a plan to control each cause.

"For example, our negative self image can be overcome with positive affirmations, or by doing good deeds, or by constantly reviewing our good points. We can overcome guilt with forgiveness. We can ask the people we've hurt to forgive us. We can ask God to forgive us. Most importantly, we can forgive ourselves."

"How about my fear of success?" Al asked.

"If we have a fear of success, we can overcome it by creating small successes and focusing on those successes. We can go back to work and be an asset to our employer. We can take an education course or start some project and work hard to complete it. We can make a point to review those successes each morning and each evening. That way we become comfortable with success and seek it out.

"Regarding drugs, if we can stay on top of our emotions, then severe emotions won't cause us to medicate them with drugs. If we have extreme emotions, we can recognize them, name them, establish their cause, determine if they are encouraging us to take action, and whether that action is good for us. If we still can't get them under control, we can call our sponsor."

"All this requires a lot of work," Juan observed.

"Yes it does," Bill said. "Our SDB has been developing since childhood and has become a life- long habit; so we can't expect to control it by making a few quick changes. We need to end our old habit of reactive decisions, and start a new habit of well thought through decisions."

"Well," Juan said, "it looks like I have a lot more work to do. How do we identify the cause or causes of our SDB?"

"A good starting point," Bill said, "is by examining our negative self image. At the next meeting we can start on it."

Chapter 28 – SDB Part III

The meeting started and Bill said to Juan, "Today we're going to try to help you find the causes of your SDB. I think you should first determine which actions were self destructive? For instance, was leaving the foster family self destructive?"

"Well," Juan said, "I had a chance at the foster home to settle down and follow the rules, but I guess I was used to living without rules – without people telling me what to do. At Juvie there were too many rules, and I hated following them."

"I know what you mean," Al said. "Like you, I didn't have many rules either when I was young. I liked it that way. Even today, whenever I run into a rule I don't like, I try to get around it or over it or past it in some way. Maybe that has something to do with my SDB."

"Well," Juan said, "I hadn't thought of it that way. Maybe my SDB was also rooted in the fact that I didn't want to follow rules. I thought my SDB was selling drugs or joining the gang. I knew selling drugs might put me in jail, but at the time I didn't care if I got in trouble."

"That's interesting," George said. "Why didn't you care if you got in trouble?"

"I don't know," Juan responded. "As I think back on it, it seems like being arrested by the police was almost pleasant compared to the way my family treated me. At least the police didn't beat me up. Most people might think that getting myself arrested was self destructive, and it was. But it was much less painful then being at home."

"You know," Al said, "I didn't care if I got in trouble either. And as I think about it, I don't know why. I spent a good part of my childhood being angry. Getting in trouble may have been a way of getting back at the thing that was making me angry. It was like I wanted to make a statement. I wanted to tell everyone I was mad. But who was I angry at? My mother? The neighbors? The school? I don't know, maybe everything in my life. Maybe that's why I broke rules. It was a way of hurting those people who had hurt me. Maybe I was trying to get back at the whole world for what it had done to me."

"I can see that," Juan said. "I've had some of those same feelings. I was angry at my dad and brothers, but at the same time, it felt like I was angry at something bigger. Just like you said, I think I was angry at the whole world, too. It was like everyone else had it better than I did. They had good families. Why didn't I? It seemed so unfair, and I wanted to get revenge."

"Unfair!" George said. "That's exactly the way I felt back then. Everything was unfair. Everyone else had real moms and dads; I was in foster. Life was unfair, the world was unfair, and I spent a lot of time angry. I had a good friend in school who invited me to his house a lot, and one day he asked if he could come to my house. I didn't want him to know I was in foster, so I told him no. That made me feel bad, and I got mad at myself and mad at the world. And all I could think about was how unfair my life was. I remember kicking everything in sight on the way home."

"You know," Al said, "it's interesting that we all were mad at something outside of ourselves. But somehow we thought that we could get back at it by hurting ourselves. Were we angry at ourselves? Did we feel it was our fault we were worthless and deserved the treatment others gave us?"

"If you recall," Bill said, "a while back we talked about SDB as a means of coping. For example, here in prison, what do you do if the food is bad?"

"We complain to the officer," Al said.

"Right," Bill said. "What can he do about it?"

"Nothing," Al said. "He doesn't make the menu or cook the food. He just brings it.

"But you complain anyway," Bill said. "Your complaining is a means of coping – you are coping with a situation you can't change. Coping is normal; it's what we do when we can't solve a problem.

"As humans, it's in our nature to solve problems. But when a difficulty is bothering us, and our hands are tied and we can't fix it, we get upset and frustrated. We want to reduce our upset, and we do so by coping. Complaining about the food is a means of coping; it's a way of reducing our frustration. If we yell and scream and rant and rave at someone, like the officer, our cellie, maybe even the walls, it's a way of reducing the negative emotions that are overwhelming us. It won't change the situation, but it will help to reduce our emotions a bit.

"Also, feelings of worthlessness can bring on depression. So we use coping as a way of staving off depression. We act up in some way to cope with or distract ourselves from the depression.

"I see what you mean," Al said, "I think that's what I did. I learned to cope with my feeling of worthlessness by acting up; by being disruptive in school and by breaking things – I broke the neighbor's window and threw away my mother's stuff. I was coping with my worthlessness, trying to make it go away and trying to keep the depression at bay. But my actions made me feel guilty and increased my sense of worthlessness."

"I can see that," George said, "we feel worthless, we cope with our worthlessness by causing problems, and that makes us feel we deserve punishment. Then we punish ourselves through self destructive behavior."

"Yes," Donardo said. "I see now that my crazy driving was a way of coping with my anger. As a kid I felt stupid because of my dyslexia. So, when I got in a fight with my wife, and she told me I was stupid, it just confirmed what I already believed; that nobody would want me because I was stupid. It hurt my feelings deeply and I got really angry."

"Right," Bill said. "Your crazy driving was a means of coping with your enraged emotions. If you drove crazy, maybe the hurt would go away."

"So," Al observed, "it appears that a large part of our negative image resulted from being belittled when we were young by people who were important to us. We soaked up their putdowns like little sponges and concluded we were worthless. We acted up and misbehaved as a way of coping with our feelings of worthlessness. That behavior brought on guilt, and made us feel we caused our worthlessness. So we punished ourselves for our bad behavior by being self destructive."

"Perhaps," Juan said, "we got in the bad habit of punishing ourselves for our worthlessness as kids, and we are still reacting that way as adults."

"All these thoughts are good," Al said, "but we're describing some pretty insane behavior."

"I agree," George said. "When you think about it, SDB is insane. It's insane to purposely hurt ourselves. The basic concept is crazy."

"Yes," Al said, "but we've been able to discover some of the reasons why we self destruct. And that can help us to control our SDB in the future."

Chapter 29 – Juan's Final Plan

The group gathered and Juan said, "I'd like to show you my final plan. My main goal is to completely change my life. I need to work on the following:

- New friends
    - Find a church
- A job
    - Become a skilled carpenter

- A home
    - New apartment and neighborhood
- A vehicle
    - My uncle's old Chevy
- My family
    - Join a church
- Find support
    - Church
    - NA
    - Sponsor
    - Pastor
- Acknowledge emotions
    - Emotional journal each night
    - Mantra
    - Emotions running high
        - Recognize high emotions
        - Name emotions
        - Determine the cause
        - Are they pushing me to take action?
        - Is that action good for me?
        - Put emotions in perspective
        - Call sponsor
        - No decisions
        - No drugs
- Improve self image
    - Affirmations – positive self talk
    - Assets – review my good traits
    - Wish list – change and improve my life for the better
    - Be the hero of my life
- Why do I self destruct?

- Jail seems preferable to home
- I feel worthless and deserve punishment

"OK," Bill said, "that looks like a good plan. Does anyone have any comments?"

George spoke up, "You've got 'church' in there quite a bit. My foster brother, John, joined a church when he got out, and it worked out pretty well for him."

"I've never joined a church," Juan said, "so I don't know how it works. But I do know that I can't go back to my old neighborhood or friends, so I'm planning to join a church – maybe I'll find some new friends there. What was John's experience?"

Chapter 30 – John's Story

"Well," George said. "John had been in prison three times – two for bank robberies in California and one for drugs, here in Texas. When he wrote me he was about to be paroled, I wrote back and asked him what he planned on doing, and if he'd set any goals for his life? He said he had five goals.

John's Plan

"First, he was planning to put God first in his life. He had found God in prison, and he wanted to devote his life to Him. Second, he was going to try to follow Christ's teachings and look to Him for decisions. Third, since he had spent most of his life hanging with the wrong people, he was planning to join a church and start hanging with the right people. Fourth, he was going to pursue work as a handyman or remodeler. Prior to his time in prison, he had been a carpenter and was skilled with his hands. While in prison, he had learned how to do electrical work, plumbing, and wood working. His goal was to be the best handyman he could be, and to go the extra mile for his boss or customer. Fifth, he was determined to spend a few hours every week helping the needy. Volunteers had come to the prison and had helped him discover God's love, and he wanted to help others in the same way.

"So, he was paroled, went to Houston and immediately joined a church. He attended all of the church's activities and told everyone he was looking for work. In a week's time, he was offered a job in Gulf Vista fixing up a beach house.

"The first thing he did when he arrived in Gulf Vista was to join a church. He told the pastor that he was available to help anyone in need. Then he started his new job fixing up the vacation house. The owner paid him $150.00 a week in salary and allowed him to live in the home while he worked on it.

"One day, when John was at church, the preacher asked him if he would help an elderly lady named Anita, who was having problems with her plumbing. John went to the home. Anita was very old and very poor. None of the sinks worked, the shower drain was plugged and the toilet was out of order. None of the windows and doors were opening or closing properly. John worked in the house for three days, fixing the plumbing and many other things that were out of order.

"The next Sunday, Anita told everyone at the church about all the good things John had done, and about how nice he was. Word spread, and in a short time, John had many jobs. But at every job, he did more than the customer asked, and he always charged fair prices. In addition, John volunteered to become an usher at the church. It was well known in Gulf Vista that John had been in prison, but his actions earned him a reputation for being honest, caring, and helpful.

"One day, one of the leaders of the church invited John to dinner. This fellow owned an oil service business in town. He invited John home because he wanted John to meet his daughter, Nancy.

"To make a long story short, John and Nancy started dating, and a few months later they got married. Nancy writes me frequently to tell me how she and John are doing.

"In one letter, Nancy told a story about her parents inviting them to their houseboat one Sunday after church. John said he couldn't go because he had volunteered to help a disabled woman with some repairs on her house. John asked Nancy's dad if he wanted to help him with the work, then they would be able to go on the boat sooner. Nancy's dad was not excited about the idea, but her mom suggested that all of them help with the work.

"So they all went to the woman's house, and started working. When Nancy's dad saw the condition of the house, he asked some of his employees to come and help. Five more people joined in the effort, and by late afternoon, the home had been put back into good order. Then Nancy's dad invited everyone for a party on the houseboat, including the lady whose home they had repaired.

"Nancy said that everyone had a great time because they felt wonderful about helping someone in need. She said she was proud of John because he had helped make

Gulf Vista a more loving, caring community by showing others, especially her father, the joy of helping the needy.

"In another letter, Nancy told me a story about a phone call she received from John one morning. After reminding her of his conviction for bank robbery in California, he asked her to guess where he was working that day? It turns out he was fixing the alarm at the bank!

"Another day, as Nancy was out walking the dog, John drove by, honked his horn, and waved. There happened to be two young boys walking in front of Nancy, and she overheard one of them say, 'There goes John Hanson. When I grow up I want to be just like him.'

"So, it seems that all of John's successes began by joining a church. He got his first job after he joined the church in Houston. He helped at the Gulf Vista church, and earned a good reputation there. He was introduced to his wife through that church, and most of his jobs came from church members. So, the church option worked well for him."

"Well," Bill said, "that's a good story. I agree that the church was a big help, but there were some other things that John did which also helped. First, he said he was going to follow the teachings of Christ. This is known as having a moral plan; a set of rules to follow that will give him guidance. This is very important.

"In previous meetings we talked about how most of us grew up without rules. We didn't like rules nor did we want to follow them. But if we don't have some kind of code of conduct that we can hold ourselves to, it will be difficult for us to stay out. We have to set a specific standard of behavior for ourselves before we leave here.

We need to set clear guidelines for ourselves which will help to direct and control our lives. We have to agree with these principles, and commit to ourselves to follow them.

"We expect others to follow the rules so they won't hurt us or interfere with our freedoms. Therefore, we should follow the rules and not interfere with their freedoms. We need to treat others the way we want them to treat us. And I believe that is something Jesus asked us to do.

"Second, John wanted to be an exceptional worker. If we expect to get and keep a job, it will be good for us to be positive about our work. John set a goal to be the best repair man in the city. That is very positive – positive for both his work and his attitude. If John truly enjoys the work he is doing, it will be easier for him to like himself, and thus have a good self image. And, if he is doing a good job, his work skills will always be in demand. Doing more than we are asked is called going the extra mile. And I think that is also something Jesus asked us to do.

"Third, John wanted to help others. We all want to be heroes, and when we help those in need, we become heroes. We can look at helping others as making amends, or payback for the negative things we have done. So as we help others, we help ourselves, and it's very good for our self image.

"So, at the center of John's plan were these goals – have a moral guide, join a church, be a great worker, and help others. And it worked very well for him. Thank you, George, for sharing that.

Chapter 31 – Turning Things Around

"John was able to set good goals and turn things around. Are we ready to turn things around for ourselves? What are our goals?"

"I never had any goals," Juan said. "No dreams to be someone important, like a doctor."

"I can identify with that," George said. "It's sad that I never had any goals. I wonder why?

"Maybe," Al said, "it's because we were in an endless battle just to survive. Maybe survival was our goal."

"Consider this," Bill said. "Psychologist Carl Jung was the founder of analytical psychology. He said, 'The world will ask you who you are, and if you don't know, the world will tell you.' Do we know who we are? Or better yet, do we know who we want to be? Are we letting our traumatic childhoods determine our identity?

"Up to this point we have allowed life's situations to influence our choices and the direction of our lives. But we can change; we can create a new direction for ourselves. Where do we see ourselves in five years?

"I hope," Al said, "that I don't find myself back here in five years."

"I agree," Bill said. "You know Socrates said, 'A life without purpose is not worth living.' So what's our purpose? What's our dream? What's our goal? Let's take time this week to see if we can find a dream inside our heart. And if we can, let's use that dream to create some great goals for our lives. There is no more exciting life than a focused person taking action."

Chapter 32 - Donardo's Image

At the next meeting, Donardo spoke up, "After you talked about improving our self image, I wrote down some of my negative images, and after each one I wrote something positive, an affirmation. If you don't mind, I'll read them.

N: (**Negative Image**) My reckless driving was a terrible thing.

A: (**Affirmation**) No, it was bad but not terrible.

N: I shouldn't have acted that way.

A: Where is it written that I will always act correctly? No one is perfect. Everyone makes mistakes. I can make amends.

N: I am a bad person.

A: No. Making poor choices does not make me a bad person. The many good things I do far outweigh the few bad ones.

N: The people I love hate me.

A: No, they still love me. They dislike my poor choices, but if I can change, they will forgive me.

N: I am bad, and I am going to hell.

A: No. God made me, and He doesn't make junk, He makes precious beings. He has already forgiven me.

"Very good," Bill said. "Allow me to suggest one more thing. If we make the same poor choice again and again, we're in a bad habit and we need to find a way to change it."

Chapter 33 - Addiction

At the next meeting Bill said, "Today I want to talk about addiction. How many here suffer from alcohol or drug addiction?"

Al, George, and Juan, raised their hands.

Bill said, "Some people can get seriously addicted to alcohol, while others do not. In fact, far more people are addicted to alcohol than any other drug. Marijuana is not considered addictive, but is considered a gateway to addictive drugs. All narcotic drugs are highly addictive, including many prescription drugs like Vicodin and OxyContin. If we are addicted to alcohol and we start drinking, or if we start on a narcotic drug, we only have four possible outcomes: recovery, incarceration, insanity or death.

"Once we start on drugs, our body increases its tolerance to the drug, and we need more and more of the drug to maintain the same high. Pretty soon our drug dosage is so high and so expensive we have to resort to crime to satisfy our habit – and we wind up in prison. For example, in order to get a fix, Al had to be in a drive-by shooting.

"If we have enough money to take drugs indefinitely, they will damage our brain to a point where it can no longer function rationally or sanely. This deterioration will continue, and eventually we will die. Richard Prior set himself on fire in 1980 in a drug induced psychosis. He continued on drugs daily, and by 1987 was incapable of working. He was confined to a wheelchair and died a few years later.

"As we grow physically, our decision making system matures and improves. But the use of drugs has the tendency to halt this growth. If a teen starts taking drugs at 16, by the time he is 20, he will probably still have a decision making maturity of only 16. His decision making maturity has been arrested; it has been on hold during his drug years.

"The only intelligent option for addiction is recovery. The financial situation of most addicts requires them to resort to crime to support their habits. Wealthy addicts who take drugs for long periods of time go insane and die. So we have to remember that if we take drugs or if we are alcoholic and we drink, we only have four options: recovery, incarceration, insanity or death. That's why we are here working hard on our recovery."

Chapter 34 – Control versus Rules

Al spoke up, "In previous meetings we talked about how we disliked following rules. At the last meeting you talked about a moral code – following a set of rules we establish for ourselves. I like that idea, because if I continue to disregard the rules, I'm coming back here. So I'm going to put together my own moral code that will keep me within society's rules. But the question is, why don't we like rules?"

"Well," Juan said, "When I follow someone's rules, they have control over me. When I was little, the people who had control over me were always hurting me. So I ran away from their control, and I think I'm still running. In both Juvie and foster they had rules. It's not that those places were bad, but if I followed their rules, then they were in control. Maybe that's why I left the gang – even they had rules. I guess having control of my life was more important than knowing where my next meal was coming from."

"You're right," Al said, "most of us wanted to get out of the negative situations we were in. We felt helpless and desperately wanted some control."

"I agree," George said, "but when we got control, we didn't know how to use it. It was probably because our decision making was messed up by our crappy childhoods."

"Or," Bill said, "it might be subconscious instructions. As kids we reacted to stressful situations in an immature manner and then as adults, we reacted to the same situations in the same childish ways – subconscious instructions."

"Exactly," George said. "As adults, we allowed our juvenile habits to influence our decisions. We wanted to have control, yet as adults we didn't know how to control ourselves. So we fell back on the defenses we developed as kids. We were using the thinking of a stressed out 10 year old, instead of using mature thinking – and that's why we're in here today."

"Well put," Bill said. "And that's why we need to have a plan for our lives – a plan that keeps us within the rules. We need some kind of guide, a form of self discipline, in order to stay within society's rules.

"In John's story, he decided to follow the teachings of Christ as his moral code. If we also want to stay out of prison, it's very important that we create a moral plan that keeps us within society's boundaries, and we need to commit to ourselves to follow that plan."

"I agree," George said, "we have to realize that our juvenile habits don't work for us as adults. And if we allow that kind of thinking to control our lives, then we will continue coming back here."

"Very true," Bill said. "Children who were raised in a home with logical, consistent rules developed logical and consistent thinking. We didn't have that privilege. Trying to make logical decisions with a brain that developed in an illogical environment is not easy. It does not come automatically; it's like a handicap, and we need to be aware of our limitations. If we want to control our lives, we have to set basic guidelines for controlling our decisions. In other words, each of us needs to establish a set of rules to live by."

Chapter 35 – George's Story

At the next meeting, George said, "I'm in here because of something that happened to me that I just don't understand."

"Tell us about it," Bill said.

"Well, I fell in love with a girl, and she loved me too. Her name was Sheryl. We lived together for a while, and I was never happier. She talked about getting married and having kids, and I thought it would be great to do those things. But one morning I woke up scared to death about our relationship, and I didn't know why. I told her I couldn't live with her anymore, and I left.

"Once out of the house, my fear was replaced with sadness, loneliness, and guilt for breaking her heart. My heart was broken, too. So, I did what I always did when I was down – I got drunk. That night I was arrested for public intoxication, and my probation was revoked. So now I'm here; and I still can't figure out why I walked out on the perfect woman."

"Could you give us a little more info about your life?" Bill asked.

"Well," George said, "my mom was a teenager when she had me. But CPS took me away from her when I was nine. They said she was an unfit mom.

"Mom would visit me in foster. She came a number of times and told me she was coming to get me and take me home – but she never did. She made endless promises, but never fulfilled them. I felt sad and disappointed. After a while I realized she would never bring me home.

"When you lived with her," Bill asked, "how did she treat you?"

"Most of the time, she was good to me. But there were times when she would kind of go crazy and do a lot of bad things. She would yell, call me names, and sometimes beat me. One time she was beating me with a yard stick, and it broke in half, so she grabbed a wire coat hanger and hit me with it. There were so many bruises that the school called CPS, who took me away from her."

"Did you love her?" Bill asked.

"Yes, I did. Whenever I was feeling low, I would dream of us living together in a nice home. I imagined her being there for me."

Bill asked, "Did you ever have a relationship with any other women, besides Sheryl?"

"I dated a few girls when I was in high school, but never really fell in love with anyone – not like I did with Sheryl. But why did I run, what was I afraid of?"

"My guess is," Bill replied, "that you were afraid that she might stop loving you. And if she did, you would be devastated. Not wanting to face that possibility, you ran away. The only other person you had ever loved was your mother, and she had let you down. That broke your heart, and you didn't want to get your heart broken again.

"If we fall in love with a girl, we in effect, give her control of our most precious emotion, our love. It's like giving her a piece of our heart. Can we trust that she will treat our love well? If we have given our love to others, and if they treated it poorly, we will be reluctant to give it away again.

"You loved your mother; you gave her all your love but she didn't cherish that love. She broke endless promises and it hurt you deeply. And the sad result was that it left you reluctant to share your heart with anyone else. So, when Sheryl showed you love and you started to love her, it scared you. When you saw yourself giving away your deepest emotion, you felt you couldn't trust anyone with that much of you, so you ran away.

"I understand what you are saying," George said. "I need to think about this for a while."

Chapter 36 - Guilt

Donardo said, "My mom saw on the internet that many inmates carry around a lot of guilt."

"Yes," Bill said, "guilt is one of the underlying causes of incarceration. Our conscience is the part of our mind that moralizes. It lays a guilt trip on us if we do something wrong. For example, Al broke the neighbor's window. He initially felt a rush, but in time he felt guilty about his actions which led to sadness and depression. The problem with guilt is that if we don't deal with it, it can bring on other negative emotions.

"When we do something bad, the best thing we can do is try to undo the misdeed or make amends in some way. This will help relieve our guilt. But Al was a little boy and wasn't mature enough to know how to make amends.

"If we can't make amends, then our guilt will remain in our subconscious, degrading our self image and threatening us with depression. Some of us react to this oncoming depression by throwing ourselves into our work – it's a way of diverting our attention away from those emotions. That's what Al did. He got an air conditioning job and started a used car business to divert his mind away from the memories of his traumatic childhood – memories laced with guilt and depression. He was succeeding, but the more he succeeded, the more he felt he didn't deserve the success. That's because he wasn't working to succeed, he was working to avoid the feelings of guilt and sadness."

"Of course!" Al broke in, "It all makes sense now! That's exactly it, the more I succeeded, the more I felt I didn't deserve the success. I thought I was working hard to succeed at building a new life. But in fact I was working to distract my mind away from my guilt. I should have felt good, but instead I felt bad, and that's why my emotions were all mixed up."

"I agree," Bill said. "I think you've figured out why you took drugs."

"Right," Al said, "all these months of hard work is finally paying off."

"Exactly," Bill said, "You've learned that there are causes for our actions, and if we look hard enough into our past, we can find out what those causes are. You've also learned that the answers are locked in your own mind, waiting for you to unlock them. This is an important moment."

"Yes," Al said, "I was working to run away from my guilt – but that didn't fix it. The A/C work, my used car business, the sports – none of them could fix my guilt. No matter what work I did, I felt bad inside."

"I think," George said, "it's great that Al's figured out his problem, but how can he fix it?"

"OK," Bill said, "We talked about this before. Our emotions are in turmoil, what do we do?"

"Right," George said, "I see where you're going. First, we realize our emotions are struggling. Then we give them a name, then determine their cause, see if they're trying to get us to take action, and is that action in our best interest?"

"Right," Al said. "Let's imagine this happens to me again. I feel that no matter what I do I'm miserable. Even though I'm succeeding at A/C and other things, I'm depressed. OK, I've named it – depression. So, what's causing it? Is something bad happening right now? No, I'm succeeding, things in my life are good – this isn't bad, this is good, I should feel good. But I feel bad. So something in the past is probably causing my negative emotions.

"Maybe my negative image doesn't like the fact that I'm succeeding. But my negative image was caused by others; so I'm not worthless. But still I feel bad inside. Maybe it's because I reacted poorly to my situation when I was young. I destroyed stuff and hurt people. Maybe if I apologized to those I hurt – maybe I'd feel better."

"You're going great," Bill said, "Continue."

"OK," Al said, "Maybe the first person I need to make peace with is my mother. I think about her a lot. I realize she caused most of my problems and I was hurt by what she did. But I feel badly about what I did to her, and I don't like being angry with her. I think I'll write her a letter and tell her how I feel – tell her I'm sorry for my anger and my behavior. And I can do the same for anyone else that I can find that I may have hurt. Maybe then these negative feelings will go away."

"That's good," Bill said. "I think you're on the right track. I think it would be good to start corresponding with your mother and for the two of you to start dealing with your issues together. It certainly can't hurt.

"Your story is an excellent example of fear of success, or 'success phobia,' as psychologists call it. If we are doing something good and we feel badly about it, that is an emotional red flag, and we need to stop what we are doing and start examining our feelings. Success phobia is quite common but seldom diagnosed. My guess is that half the people in the world suffer from success phobia to some degree – and most of it is caused by guilt."

"So," George said, "it looks like we are always at risk of self destruction if we have a lot of guilt in our past."

"Exactly," Bill said. "Guilt is at the center of our negative self image. That is why improving our image is so important. We'll continue with Al's self image at our next meeting."

Chapter 37 - Al's Self Image

At the next session Al said, "One of the main parts of my plan to stay out is working on my self image. My negative image was caused by the difficulties of my childhood and by the guilt for my bad behavior. I've written these things down.

"But I've also written down something positive after each negative item to help improve my image. For example, Negative (N) I was rejected and felt worthless; Positive (P) but my boss accepted me and I was an asset to the company. (N) I skipped school and dropped out; (P) but I learn fast, and I mastered air conditioning in one year. (N) I joined a gang and sold drugs; (P) but I've got a new life now without gangs and drugs. (N) I've hurt a lot of people including those I love; (P) but I can find many of those people and ask them for forgiveness.' I read these statements every day.

"I've also written down how I want to act in the future, and I read that every day, too. For instance I wrote, 'I'm going to join a church and be active. I'm going to attend NA every week. I'm going to surround myself with good friends. I'm going to reject alcohol and drugs. I'm going to talk to myself about my emotions throughout the day. I'm going to ask forgiveness from anyone I've hurt. I'm going to try to iron things out with my mother. I'm going to try to show love by helping others. I'm going to find the people who have helped me and thank them. I'm going to set a goal and work toward it. And every day I'm going to take time to cherish the good memories of my life."

"Well," Bill said, "that's pretty good. Is that your whole plan?"

"Oh, no," Al said. "That's just how I'm going to deal with my self image. I still have to address three more items; emotions, support and SDB. But I feel I've got a good handle on my self image."

"I agree," Bill said. "You are going in the right direction. You are improving your thinking. And maybe this is a good time to start talking about changing and improving our thinking.

Chapter 38 - Improving Our Thinking

"A while back we talked about our thinking structure being designed by life's experiences. Since life's many experiences are imperfect, our thinking system develops imperfectly. So we need to rebuild our thinking and decision making systems.

"Our thinking structure determines how thoughts run through our mind, how we make decisions, and how we live our lives. It determines our likes and dislikes, our priorities, our desires, our reactions, our emotions, and every other aspect of the way we think and live. No two thinking systems are the same, but all start out basically the same on the day we are born.

"When we enter this world, very little of our brain is developed. Most of the development comes from living life. It develops as we grow and as we learn activities and skills. But the part of the brain that thinks and makes decisions develops through our experiences with life. These endless experiences occur throughout our youth, all helping to build our thinking system.

"In effect, our thinking structure is designed by life. But, since life is imperfect and life's ordeals are imperfect, our thinking structure develops imperfectly. The evidence of this is the mistakes we make and the unhappiness we suffer.

"Most of our thinking structure develops during our youth, so if our youth is dysfunctional, our thinking system develops dysfunctionally. This has led us to a life of incarceration."

"So what can we do about it," Al asked.

"Our job here in counseling," Bill explained, "is to discover the defects in our thinking system and develop tools to rebuild and overcome them. We don't have to accept the thinking system given to us by life's random experiences; we can design a new logical thinking system of our own. We can reinvent our thinking, and in the process, we can reinvent ourselves. We can start by changing our thinking from negative into positive.

Chapter 39 – Positive Thinking

"There's a method of thinking called Cognitive Behavioral Therapy. It's based on the idea that we can change the way we think. Those of us who struggle with a negative self image and SDB have a habit of thinking negatively. So, it's important to start thinking positively if we hope to succeed in staying out.

"Cognitive Behavioral Therapy encourages us to work on our thinking patterns. If we can become aware of our thinking and focus on it – we can control it. We can change our thinking from negative to positive. We can be aware of negative thoughts when they occur, and then reverse them before they cause us problems.

"When we discussed emotions, I suggested that we talk to ourselves throughout the day as a way of continually monitoring our emotions. Positive thinking gives us positive emotions. Most of us don't realize that it is within our power to control both our thinking and our emotions. We just have to make the decision to do so.

"Do you remember my friend who was in the slow line at the store and his frustration was encouraging him to leave the store? Life's events continually try to push our thinking and our emotions into negative territory. And sadly, we are in a bad habit of allowing life to do that to us. That's because we are using the thinking structure given to us by life's random events rather than rebuilding our thinking structure to our own specifications. And we can rebuild it by getting in the good habit of continually asking ourselves, 'is my thinking positive? Are my emotions positive?'

"We also talked about mantra. My mantra is 'love everyone, accept everything, enjoy every moment.' It is the difference between me having a day of frustration versus a day of peace.

"We all have defective thinking structures which developed during childhood. But it is within our power to rebuild those thinking structures. We can do that by talking to ourselves continually about our thinking and our emotions. We can do it by adopting a mantra and living by it.

Chapter 40 – Changing Beliefs

"Also, our beliefs can affect our thinking and how we react to events. We need to examine our beliefs and make sure they are realistic. For example, as a child, Al felt his mother should have been there for him. He saw other moms at home with their kids and he felt he should be treated the same. In other words, he believed that life should be fair. Therefore, when his mom wasn't there, he reacted by destroying things. But was Al's belief realistic? Can we expect life to be fair? No. We want it to be fair, but in actuality, many times life is not fair. Sometimes moms are negligent.

"So Al got angry at Thanksgiving and threw away his mother's beets because he felt life should be fair, when in fact it wasn't. If he had believed life isn't fair he wouldn't have destroyed things. The key here is that it's the 'belief,' not the 'event,' that initiated the difficulties.

"Think of it this way, two thirteen year old boys are seduced by older women. One thinks it's the greatest thing that ever happened to him while the other is traumatized by it. It's a matter of what we believe that determines how we react.

"If Al or any of us want to live a normal life, we need to bring our beliefs in line with the real world, and realize that life is not fair. So, if we are rejected, we can say to ourselves, 'That's too bad, but sometimes life is unfair, and this is one of those times.' We can find our support person and vent our feelings. They will help us keep things in perspective. Also, we might say, 'I'm feeling rejected and sad, so maybe I'll go help someone, and that will help me feel better.' If our beliefs are rational, our emotions will stay in control.

"The rational belief, 'life is not fair,' helps to keep us in charge of our emotions. Continuing the irrational belief, 'life should be fair,' could provoke feelings of anger and resentment when life treats us unfairly. If we react badly, as Al did, it will eventually bring on guilt, and our self image will be damaged. So, it's important to keep our beliefs rational and our thinking and actions positive."

"I understand what you mean," Al said, "but most of my negative image came from the fact that my mother was not there for me – even on the holidays. Parents should be there for their kids."

"Yes," Bill said, "we would hope all parents would be able to raise their kids properly. But the reality is that some parents are unwilling or unable to do so. Is it fair? No, but it's the way things are in the real world.

"Here's something else to think about. If someone hurts us, should we react to what he/she has done by hurting ourselves?"

"No," Al said, "that's not logical."

"Right," Bill said, "but we do hurt ourselves. We have a history of hurting ourselves when others have hurt us. We're in a bad habit. So it's important for us to change our thinking in order to break that habit. We can say, 'someone hurt me, so I need to go talk to my sponsor.' If we can change our thinking, it will greatly improve our lives. Does anyone else feel they were hurt as a child?"

"Yeah," George said, "I was treated horribly by my mom's boyfriend. He hated me and did everything in his power to make my life miserable. He was always slapping the side of my head. He told me I was garbage, and that I'd be in prison one day. I kick myself everyday for letting him be right. Here was a grown man terrorizing a little boy. If it had been up to me, he'd be the one in prison."

"Well," Bill said, "you've got some pretty strong feelings about that. Do you get angry when you think about the way he treated you?"

"Of course I do," George said. "Wouldn't you be angry if that happened to you? I was angry then and I still get angry when I think about it."

"I know just where you are coming from," Juan said. "I've been there. I had the anger, the negative image, the worthless feeling. I used drugs to feel better – I know what it's like."

"Right," George said, "And it was wrong of him to do that. I don't care what you say about life not being fair. He was wrong and he should be the one being punished – not me."

"I agree," said Al. "And when you talk about life not being fair, it seems like you are saying that it was OK for those people to abuse us. We were just kids – they should have treated us better."

"So," Bill said, "it seems like these remembrances have brought up a lot of anger. But what are we really angry at?"

Juan said, "I think it's like Al said, it seems that you are defending the people that hurt us. They caused our negative self image and the need to escape our lives through drugs – they caused us to be here. Was it OK for them to do that?"

"No, not at all," Bill said. "I think that their actions were deplorable, and society feels the same way. When society finds situations like yours they generally remove the children from the parents – which is what happened to you, George. But in reality, the abuse did happen, and you reacted to it, and you're still reacting to it. But who did your reactions hurt?"

"I'm not sure what you mean," Al said. "Do you mean like hurting other people or destroying stuff?"

"Who went to prison?" Bill asked.

"Why, we did," Al said.

"So, they hurt you and you reacted by eventually hurting yourself. And the question is how will you respond in the future when something unfair happens? Not "if" something unfair happens, but "**when**" something unfair happens – because life is not fair – and something unfair "**will**" happen to all of us some time in the future. How will we respond? Our habit has been to hurt ourselves. Are there other options?"

"Of course," George said, "there are other options. I don't want to go to prison again. That serves no purpose."

"Very good," Bill said. "Then what do we do?"

"Well," Al said, "I think what you're trying to tell us is that we need to start accepting the idea that life will not be fair."

"Exactly," Bill said, "It's imperative to have accurate beliefs in our heads – ideas of how the world really is, versus how we would like it to be. There will always be tragedies in life. We'll have fights with people we love. Loved ones will die. We will lose our job. There will be unfair heartbreaks throughout our lives. If we respond to them with SDB, we might just as well never leave here.

"Do we stop living our lives because the future won't be perfect? No. So if we realize that tragedies are a part of life, then extreme emotions will be less likely to drive us to SDB. If we are armed with the right tools to deal with severe emotions, we will have a better chance of surviving life's difficulties."

Donardo asked, "Would tragedies be another reason to have support?"

"That's a perfect example," Bill said, "life's tragic events are probably the most important reasons we need to have support. They cause extreme negative emotions, like distress, heartbreak, and grief. It's imperative that we have strong, stable support when our heart is broken. It's when we're most vulnerable to SDB."

Chapter 41 - Financial Maturity

The group convened and Bill said, "When we were in the free world, did we get our paycheck, cash it and blow the money? Or did we go to the bank, put 10% in savings and the rest in checking to be used only as needed?"

Donardo said, "Blowing the paycheck is how I lived before I got married."

"Me too," said George. "I lived from paycheck to paycheck."

"I opened a checking account," Al said, "but I never saved very much."

"Our goal here is to put together a plan to stay out," Bill said. "We are trying to move away from a decision making system we developed as an abused child and start using a system based on logic and reason.

"We can measure how far we have come by the quality of our decisions. Are we making high quality decisions guided by adult intellect, or low quality decisions driven by childhood emotions?

"A good way of measuring our progress is financial maturity. Do we rule money, or does money rule us? Do we blow our paycheck – which is a childish thing to do, or do we spend it wisely – which is a mature thing to do?"

"I have to say," George said, "that your example certainly makes a point. After you said it, I could envision myself at the bank putting some of my paycheck in savings, and the rest in checking. I see myself as very mature – very organized. Yes, that's what I would like to do. Live a life in control. I've never done that before. I went from paycheck to paycheck, and when the rent or car payment was due it would take the whole paycheck to cover it; I'd have no money for food or anything else till the next paycheck. I can see why that was immature – not well thought through at all."

"I agree" said Juan. "In my drug business we had lots of money, but we never saved it or managed it in any way. We just spent it. It was insane when you think about it."

"When I got married," Donardo said, "I was in charge of the finances. But the month they shut off our utilities my wife took charge. I had spent the money on stupid stuff. I can see now that it's good to have money in the bank to pay the bills. If we can do that, it will be evidence that we are making mature decisions – decisions based on intellect and not on juvenile emotions."

"Exactly," Bill said. "We are used to making decisions based on immature habits. Our plan is to move away from that kind of behavior. We can measure how well our plan is working by our financial maturity."

Chapter 42 - Donardo's Plan

At the next meeting Donardo said, "I have finished my plan and I would like some feedback."

"Great," Bill said, "give it to us."

"OK," Donardo said, "My main goals are:
- Change my thinking
- Practice anger management

Things I Need to Change:

1) Improve Communications – Family, Others:
- Talk to my wife about feelings
- Talk to my kids about feelings
- Talk to my counselor about feelings

2) Work on finding support:
- Church
- Sponsor
- Family
- Counselor

3) Take Charge of My Anger:
- Anger management counseling
- Start an 'Emotional Journal'

- Mantra – love everyone, love myself, accept everything and enjoy every moment
- Extreme Emotions – acknowledge upset; name the emotion; determine its cause; examine; put in perspective; go for a walk, call sponsor, no driving.

4) Work on improving my image:
- Affirmations – I am a good person
- Stop negative thinking

5) Work on my self destructive behavior (SDB):
- Anger – no actions
- Go walking
- Find support person

"Well, what do you think?"

"I like it," George said. "Your anger was your undoing, and you've addressed it throughout your plan. Have you talked to your wife about any of this?"

"Oh yes," Donardo said. "She and I write every few days and I send her all the things we talk about here. I've been sending her parts of my plan for some time now. She sends me back suggestions and she has been putting things down for herself to think about. She has lined us up a counselor we can see together, and she's already visited her once. She said it was very helpful."

"Well," Bill said, "that sounds positive – it seems like you are well on your way."

"Yes," Donardo said, "but will I actually follow my plan when I get out? That's the big question."

Chapter 43 - Amnesty

The group gathered and Bill said, "Does anyone think it's a good idea to hold on to old hurts?"

"Not me," said Juan.

"Me either," said Al.

The others agreed.

"I think we all agree," Bill said, "that nothing positive can come from holding on to old hurts. We feel anger, resentment, even hatred towards those who have hurt us. These are negative emotions and can push us into negative thinking. OK, another question, 'Are any of us perfect?'"

"No to that one too," Juan said.

"Definitely no," said Al.

The others agreed with Al and Juan. Bill said, "So none of us are immune from making mistakes and hurting others. When we do, we feel guilt, remorse and shame. So here we have another batch of negative emotions that can cause negative thinking.

"We all carry around two batches of negative emotions; one from those who have hurt us, and the other from those we have hurt. The sad result of all these negative emotions is the damage to our thinking and our self image.

"We can start removing these emotions from our thinking by using an exercise I call 'general amnesty.' Back in the Old West, if a range war was going on between ranchers, the Governor might step in and declare amnesty. Amnesty is when everyone is forgiven for their crimes. If a man had stolen another man's cattle, or burned down his home, or destroyed his fencing, then he had to go to that person, ask for forgiveness, and try to make amends, if possible. If everyone did that, then amnesty was declared, and no one was prosecuted.

But the Governor could only declare amnesty if all parties agreed to it. Everyone had to agree to stop fighting. Everyone had to agree to forgive everyone else.

"We can declare 'amnesty' in our own lives. We can ask for forgiveness from those we have hurt if we can find them. We can tell anyone who has hurt us that we were hurt by their actions, and we can forgive them. When others forgive us and when we forgive others, we bring amnesty into our lives. In effect, we make up for the bad things we have done to others by forgiving the bad things that others have done to us."

Donardo spoke up, "I know that this is not a religious group, but that's right at the center of the teachings of Christ. He asked us to forgive others, and to ask God and others to forgive us. If we can do that, God forgives us and removes our sins. I brought God into my life while I've been in here, and I've been working on forgiveness ever since. I have to tell you – I feel great peace."

"Well thank you," Bill said. "That fits right into our amnesty discussion. Anyone else?"

Al asked, "What if we can't find the people we've hurt or the people that have hurt us?"

"If we can't find the people we've hurt," Bill said, "we can find people in need and we can help them. This will make up for the hurt we've caused. If we have faith in God, we can ask Him for forgiveness. Also, we can realize that the persons we've hurt the most are probably ourselves. We can make a commitment to treat ourselves better in the future.

"In addition, we can start accepting people just as they are – faults and all. If we do this often, it will become a habit and it will be easier for us to accept and forgive people who have hurt us in the past. If we practice forgiveness and acceptance of others and ourselves, it will improve our emotions, and we'll start letting go of many of our old hurts. It will also help us to stop judging others.

Chapter 44 - Judging

"Speaking of judging, if we are trying to get our beliefs correct and thinking positive, we need to stop judging ourselves and others. Judging pushes us into negative emotional territory. When we use words like, should, must, and ought, we are judging. 'My mother should have been there.' 'I should have tried harder in school.' Instead, we can look at the big picture. 'My mom had to work two jobs and couldn't be home.' 'I had a lot of issues as a child; it was hard for me to focus at school.'

"Many times we complain about things that are out of our control – like the quality of food in prison, or the weather. It serves no purpose except to degrade our emotions. It's vital to start accepting the things we have little control over. AA says 'to accept the things we cannot change.'

"Sometimes we judge ourselves too harshly. We might say "It's terrible that I failed. I'm no good." With these harsh judgments we place unreasonable demands on ourselves, which can make us feel depressed and worthless. We have to realize that we are human and we make mistakes – everyone does; but that doesn't mean we are bad people.

"It is unreasonable to feel we won't make mistakes or hurt anyone. If we set in our minds to accept ourselves and others just the way all of us are, it will help us overcome our unreasonable old beliefs. It's time to throw away all our negative baggage. It's time to forgive ourselves and others. It's time to let go of judging."

George said, "Can you give us some examples of old beliefs?"

"Yes," Bill said, "let's look at two common irrational beliefs, 'nothing bad should ever happen to me' and 'everyone should always treat me fairly'. These irrational beliefs cause the unhealthy emotions of anger, depression, hatred, and jealousy. If we want to experience healthy emotions we need to discard these old beliefs and start creating new rational beliefs – like 'bad things will happen from time to time,' and 'people aren't perfect, so we won't always be treated fairly.'

"If we get sick and think, 'I shouldn't get sick,' we can realize this is an irrational belief because everyone gets sick sooner or later. So if we want to create a rational belief we need to align ourselves with the real world and accept the fact that sickness will happen to us once in a while. Instead of getting angry and depressed when we get sick, we can try to experience the healthier emotions of sadness and annoyance."

"So," Bill asked, "how are we going to respond when we are treated unfairly in the future?"

"Obviously," George said, "we have to start by rethinking our beliefs. We need to 'accept people more and judge them less'. We need to stop judging ourselves harshly and accept that we will make mistakes from time to time."

"And," Donardo said, "if we can learn from our mistakes, then mistakes can have a positive side. We can say, 'OK, a good thing can come from this if I learn something and work hard not to make the same mistake again.' Therefore if I get angry, I can go for a walk, rather than jump in the car and race off."

"But remember," Bill said, "If we make the same mistake over and over, it is no longer a mistake. It is a bad habit, and we need to find a way to change it."

Chapter 45 – Al's Plan

The meeting opened and Al said, "My plan is finished, but it's different from my original thinking. I have both an offensive plan and a defensive plan – kind of like a football team. My offense is my life going forward – my goals, job and hobbies. My defense is how I stay out; it's how I defend myself against everything that will try to drag me back in here.

"So my offensive plan is to go back to my old job and learn the trade backwards and forwards. Maybe my boss or fellow workers can help me find a place to live. Also, I hope to go back to playing baseball and soccer. That about covers my offensive.

"My defense plan is designed to keep me from going back to drugs or crime. It includes is Narc Anon, a church, a sponsor, and a counselor. I'm going to contact my mom and others I've hurt and try to start the healing process there. To that end, I've already written to my mom. My defense against my poor image is to affirm my assets and my successes; and to remind myself that God loves me, my friends love me, I can love myself. My defense against SDB is to recognize my strong emotions; identify them, analyze them, and deal with them.

"So what do you think?"

"I like it," Bill said, "It sounds like you have a great plan."

Chapter 46 – Leo's Success

The meeting opened and Bill said, "As you know, Leo got out a few months ago. You might remember he was here for his third DWI. Anyway, I got a letter from him, and he is doing fine. The first thing he did when he got out was join a church. He started going to AA, and he committed to 90 meetings in 90 days. Then he went back to his boss and was able to get his old job back – on probation.

"After a month out of prison, sober and doing well at work, Leo went to his wife's home and knocked on the door. His wife answered the door. He told her he had been sober for a month and had gotten his old job back. She said she wanted nothing to do with him and closed the door in his face.

"Leo didn't get angry, nor did he go off and get drunk as was his old habit. He understood why she would still have hard feelings. But instead of leaving, he sat down on the front steps and prayed that she might change her mind. He sat there praying for hours.

"When it started getting dark she came out and sat down next to him. He said, 'Do you think you could ever forgive me for all the horrible things I've done to you and our kids?' When she saw his remorse she put her arm around him and said, 'Do you know how many years I've prayed you would say those words? Yes, I forgive you. I hate what you've done, but I still love you. When I told you I wanted nothing to do with you, you didn't go off and get drunk. I didn't think you would ever change, but it seems you have.'

"Leo and his wife are building a new, better relationship. The family has started attending church together, and Leo's wife and kids have started going to Al-Anon.

"Leo was promoted at work and started a program to help other employees struggling with substance abuse. Leo and his wife are very much devoted to each other and are leaders in their church. Leo ended his letter by writing, 'There is a God, and I'm one of His miracles.' "

Chapter 47 – Anxiety

The meeting opened and Juan said, "I've had anxiety and depression from time to time. What can I do about it?"

"Anxiety," Bill explained, "is an unpleasant emotional state, the source of which is usually unidentified. It's similar to fear, but with fear we can identify the threat."

"Why am I afraid of something that I can't identify?" Juan asked.

"Because," Bill said, "the thing we are afraid of is hidden in our subconscious. Our subconscious is worried that something bad might happen to us, or that we are forgetting something important. Our job is to find that hidden concern and determine if it's serious or not.

"If we discover it is not a serious issue, then our anxiety will go away by itself. If we discover our hidden fear is a real threat, we can develop a plan to deal with it. If we implement the plan, and if we feel it has a good chance of success, then our anxiety will diminish. Most hidden fears turn out to be invalid, and once identified, go away. Almost one third of Americans suffer from anxiety."

"OK," Juan said, "so how do I determine what the fear is?"

"What I do," Bill said, "is to make a list of the worst things that can happen to me. Get killed somehow, or get a terminal disease. Become handicapped? Lose my wife, a parent or child. Go back to drugs and end up on the street. If I'm experiencing anxiety, I review these areas of my life, and if they are secure, then I can relax knowing my concern is over something small."

"I've had that," George said. "If I had an argument with someone or used harsh words, the thought of that might sit in the back of my mind and keep me worrying all day. I would think that's anxiety."

"That's a good example," Bill said. "When we have a nagging worry in the back of our mind, we can review any interactions we've had with others. If we realize there was a disagreement, then we can go to the person involved and try to resolve the issue. This usually helps relieve our anxiety."

Al said, "When I was on the street and bothered by those unknown fears, I would ask myself, 'Do I know where my next meal is coming from? Do I know where I'm going to sleep tonight?' If I knew the answers to those questions, then a lot of my fear would go away."

"Exactly," Bill said, "once we identify we are experiencing anxiety, we can go down the list of possible problems, starting with the most serious ones. And like Juan said, once we list all the worst things that can happen, and can see we are not in any imminent danger, then we can realize that the anxiety is probably from something small, and not worth worrying about right now. When we can put things in perspective, our anxiety will diminish."

"I can appreciate what you're saying," Juan said, "but I've had this anxiety all my life. I don't see it going away with a few simple thoughts."

"That's understandable," Bill said. "As a kid, you didn't know where your next meal was coming from, so you have a lot of issues to deal with, and they're not going to go away easily.

"But there are some things we can do. We can think of anxiety as a form of insecurity. Life's many unknowns can make us feel insecure. As we start removing these unknowns, like where we will work and live, our insecurity will decrease. If we can get our life into a good routine, there will be fewer unknowns, and we will feel more secure and less anxious. If our plan to stay out is solid, and if we follow it closely, our anxiety will diminish.

"Also, destructive behaviors increase anxiety while healthy behaviors decrease it; that's why it's important to follow the rules. It stands to reason that if we are breaking rules, our anxiety has to increase because our subconscious worries about the possible consequences. If we can replace destructive behaviors, like ignoring rules, with healthy behaviors, such as having and following a moral code, then our anxiety should decrease.

"Also, isolation can increase anxiety, so staying in touch with others is important. This is another good reason to have support."

"One more thing, since anxiety is an unknown worry, it is a major cause of depression, because it's depressing to worry about things – especially something unknown. But, anxiety and depression are just thoughts in our minds, and can be overcome by other thoughts – better thoughts – thoughts like committing to ourselves to follow the rules, and to follow our plan. This will reduce our anxiety. Then, when we get out of here, and actually implement our plan, and truly follow it, our anxiety and depression will leave us."

Chapter 48 – George's Plan

The meeting opened and George began, "I have my plan put together, and I wanted your input. But first, let me give you a little history. As you know, CPS took me from my mom, and I lived in foster homes most of my childhood. In my teenage years I got in more than my share of fights. I drank a little but did OK in school. I got a job at Burger King while still in high school and continued working there after graduation. I was promoted to team leader by the time I was 20.

"Most of my friends worked with me. We hung around together and partied a lot – mostly at each other's places. I was dating a lot of the girls in our group, but none seriously until Sheryl.

"I always drank at our parties. It cost me a DWI at 19, a PI at 21 and a second DWI two months later, for which I got 2 years probation. While on probation, I got another PI, so now I'm in here.

"With two DWI's and two PI's, my drinking is obviously a problem – and I have to stop. So here's my plan.

"I'm going to join AA. It will be my support, and I'm hoping to find a sponsor there. I'm going to try to get my old job back. I heard they have counseling, so that's where I'll continue to work on my emotions and self image. Between the AA and the counseling, I hope to turn my SDB around. What do you think?"

"That's a good start," Bill said, "But I have two concerns: First, your old job will put you in the midst of your old drinking buddies – your best friends. But if your best friends encourage you to go drinking with them, they're, in effect, your worst enemies. Second, if your company doesn't have a counseling program, your support is limited to AA – there's no backup. How will you deal with your emotions, self image and SDB?"

"Well," George said, "regarding job and friends, I'll have to start telling people 'no' sooner or later, because I'll probably be invited to parties from time to time. If the company doesn't have counseling, I guess I'll have to find a counselor somewhere else."

"You might want to consider a hobby," Bill said. "It will give you something to do in your off hours to keep you from being lured out to parties. Or consider some kind of outreach – some way to help others. An outreach is very positive for your self image. My worry is that your plan doesn't have a lot of depth. You have 2 DWI's and 2 PI's, but you're hanging all your hopes on AA and company counseling, which may not be there.

"Also, you may want to consider asking forgiveness from anyone you may have hurt, and forgiving those who may have hurt you – like your mom and maybe even her boyfriend if he is around. Forgiveness is a pathway to emotional healing. And it wouldn't hurt to find those who have helped you in the past, and thank them, like maybe your foster parents.

"Also, each night consider writing down the good things that happened to you that day. While you're at it, consider taking a little time remembering the good memories of your life. These are just some thoughts."

Chapter 49 – The NA Group Ends

Bill opened the meeting and said, "This week will be my last week leading our group. Next week you will have a new leader. My boss is retiring, and I've been asked to take his place. But I'll still be working here at the prison."

George said, "Wow, that's quite a change for us; we'll be sad to see you go."

"I agree," said Al, "I've felt really comfortable here."

"Thank you," Bill said. "I appreciate your kind words."

"I don't know if I can get used to someone new." George said. "I feel like I'll have to start from the beginning."

"I think you'll do just fine," Bill said. "I've known your new leader for a few years now, and he's very professional. You can give him your background, and tell him what you've learned about your image, your emotions and your SDB. Also, you can show him your plans to stay out.

"If you ever need to talk to me, just make an appointment, and I'll be happy to meet with you. I think we should stay in touch, both here in prison and especially when you get out. If you wish, I can be the information person for our group. If someone sends me something, I'll relay it to the others.

Also, and this is very important, please write me on your 2nd year anniversary of leaving here telling me where you are and what you are doing. If you run into a problem, please let me know, maybe I can help. Allow me to leave you with some thoughts on success."

Chapter 50 - Success

Success is making our state of mind more important then what we are doing.

Success is guiding our emotions toward peace, versus allowing them to be lured into turmoil.

Success is letting go of judging, controlling and needing to be right.

Success is realizing mistakes are inevitable.

Success is working to heal the wounds we have caused, and the wounds in our hearts.

Success is setting goals and using our power of choice wisely.

Success is finding a profession we like.

Success is allowing joy and peace to be more important than money and being accepted.

Success is going through a day harmlessly – hurting no one in our thoughts, words or actions; including ourselves.

Success is making the world a little better each day.

Chapter 51 – Donardo's Letters

Two months after Bill left the group, Donardo was paroled. Four months after his release he sent Bill a letter. He was home with his wife and they were seeing a counselor every week to work on their relationship and help him manage his anger. They had started to express their feelings to each other almost every day. Part of the counseling included improving his self image and monitoring his SDB. He felt he was making good progress, and he thanked Bill for all his help.

Two years after Donardo was paroled he sent Bill a letter. He was still doing well, and he and his wife were still in counseling. He said their communication was excellent, their fighting days were over, and they were madly in love with each other again. He said he was repeating his mantra daily: 'love everyone, love himself, accept everything and enjoy every moment.' He said he was enjoying life more and more each day. He said the counseling he got while in prison was the turning point of his life.

Chapter 52 – George's Letter

Seven months after George was paroled he sent Bill a letter. Sadly he was back in prison again for DWI. He returned to his job at Burger King after getting out, and had joined AA and attended meetings regularly. But after about four months, he didn't think AA was doing him any good, so he stopped attending.

From his first day at work his old crowd invited him back to the party scene. But he turned them down while going to AA. However, after dropping out of AA he finally accepted their invitation. He thought it wouldn't be a problem if he didn't drink anything. He continued partying, and after a while he convinced himself it would be OK to have one drink. He felt that his real problem was driving while drunk and made a commitment to only have one drink – and not to drive if he drank more than that.

For a while he limited his drinking to one drink per party. In time, however, he started drinking a little more, and pretty soon he was drinking heavily again. Up to this time, whenever he found himself too drunk to drive, he was able to find rides back to his apartment. Then one night, thinking he only had to drive a short distance, George tried to drive home. On the way, he hit a sign and someone wrote down his license plate number. In a short while, the police found him at his apartment – he was still drunk. He was arrested, and his probation was revoked.

George felt his mistakes were going back to his old drinking buddies, and thinking it wasn't important to have support. He had no family, and so his drinking buddies continued to be his family.

If he had told his AA group that he was having one drink per party they would have tried to talk him out of it. He could have gotten an AA sponsor or gotten counseling through his company, but he didn't think those things were important. His sponsor would have also encouraged him not to take that first drink.

Something was driving him to drink heavily, but without support he had no one to encourage him to find the reason for his drinking. Neither was there anyone to help him to address either his emotions or his self image, which were probably the cause of his heavy drinking and his SDB.

George was still in prison at the two year anniversary of his parole. He and Bill were writing to each other regularly. There was no counseling at his present prison, but he and a few other inmates in his pod had created their own AA group with the help of an AA leader's manual sent to him by Bill. Looking forward, George was scheduled to get out in a few months and stated he was really committed to following the program this time.

Chapter 53 – Juan's Letter

Five months after Juan was paroled, he sent Bill a letter. He explained in his letter that before he left prison he had been writing to a church about 'adopting' him. The church had an outreach program to help inmates transition back into the real world. They helped him find a nice apartment above a garage and had a temporary job for him. Within two weeks he found a full time job working with a landscape company.

He went to church each week and also attended a 'young singles' group. The pastor of the church was a licensed counselor and Juan started meeting with him each week to discuss his self image and his SDB. The pastor encouraged him to consider involvement in an outreach, so he started working at the church's food bank, giving out food to needy people Saturday mornings.

He started going to NA meetings his first week out. He tried three different groups before finding one he was comfortable with. One of the leaders agreed to sponsor him. He and his sponsor worked on his uncle's old car, and the two of them got it running again.

Juan told Bill he felt good about his situation and thanked him for all that he had done for him.

Two years after Juan was paroled he again wrote to Bill. He was still going to church and NA meetings weekly and met with his sponsor at least twice a month. He said he expected to do that for the rest of his life.

He had found a better paying job as a mechanic and went to the community college for an auto repair course. He graduated and got a job with a car dealer who sent him to Detroit for special training. He loved mechanic work and was good at it. His boss told him he was the 'go to' guy when it came to diagnosing auto problems.

Juan said that every day he would talk positively to himself – constantly affirming his successes and other good points. He was repeating his mantra every day throughout the day, 'my state of mind is more important than what I am doing.' He felt truly upbeat about his life going forward.

Chapter 54 – Al's Letter

Six months after Al's parole, Bill received a letter. In it, Al reported going back to his old job and that his boss was happy to have him back. A friend let him move in with him until he could find an apartment of his own.

Al joined a church where they had an NA meeting once a week. He found a sponsor there who encouraged him to start going to some of the church's activities, including a young people's group. He started attending the group and met some good people to hang around with.

Al located his mother and the two made peace with each other. He visits her regularly and sometimes they go to church together.

In keeping with his plan, Al was writing down his emotions each night and was repeating his mantra each morning, 'Do what you love. Love what you do.' He felt that his self image was improving and his emotions were stable.

Two years after Al had been paroled he wrote Bill again. He was still attending NA and meeting with his NA sponsor regularly. He was also staying in touch with his mother. His job was going well, and he was close to getting his A/C license. His boss even arranged for him to get counseling for his self image and his SDB, and he was going twice a month.

He had met a girl at church, and they were dating seriously. He was also back to playing soccer and baseball. He was still writing down his feelings each night and repeating his mantra each morning. He reported having no strong urge to do drugs again and that he felt good about his future.

<u>The End</u>
How to Stay Out 10/14/11

A New Way of Thinking

Every human thinking structure is defective. The evidence of this is the mistakes we make and the unhappiness we experience.

Our thinking structure determines how thoughts run through our mind, how we make decisions, and how we live our lives. It determines our likes and dislikes, our priorities, our desires, our reactions, our emotions, and every other aspect of the way we think and live. No two thinking systems are the same, but all start out the same, as billions of blank neurons waiting to be encoded and arranged.

When we are born, only a small amount of our brain is developed; just enough to allow us to breathe, eat, cry and so forth. The majority of our brain develops as we live life. It develops as we grow and as we learn activities like walking and talking. It develops as we learn skills such as reading and writing. But the cognitive area of our brain, the part that thinks and makes decisions, develops mostly through our experiences with life. Life's experiences also shape our emotions.

For example, shortly after birth we feel hunger and start crying. Someone feeds us, and we feel satisfied. Hunger creates crying which brings feeding which causes satisfaction – our thinking structure has started developing. All events that happen to us, such as bathing, diaper changing, recognizing faces, etc., help develop our thinking structure. As we get older we get scolded for running in the street, or praised for helping our little sister, and our thinking structure develops. Whether we are dealing with a playground bully, fishing with our dad, or lost in a store searching for our mom, endless experiences occur throughout our life, all helping to build our thinking and emotional systems.

In effect, our thinking structure is designed by life. But, since life is imperfect and life's experiences are imperfect, our thinking structure develops imperfectly. The evidence of this is the mistakes we make and the unhappiness we suffer.

But there is hope, because we don't have to accept the thinking system given to us by life's random experiences; we can design a new logical thinking system of our own.

Love, Joy and Peace

If we want our new thinking system to be the best it can be, we need to build it on life's greatest values; the values of love, joy and peace. These values are also the building blocks of our soul. We can verify this by locating their source. For example, what is the source of love; where does it come from? We know what causes hate; we hate people when they do bad things to us. But what causes love? Why do we love some people?

In the same way, we know that sadness comes when something bad happens, but where does joy come from? Or, if many difficulties occur, we are in turmoil – so we know what causes turmoil; but what causes peace? Love, joy and Peace come from within. Their seeds are planted in us at birth and they grow and mature as we grow.

Let's think about the person we love most in the world. Can we feel where our love for them comes from? Did we love them the moment we saw them, or did our love for them grow as we got to know them?

We are all born with the potential to love, and there are different kinds of love. There is romantic love, brotherly love, and the love we have for our family. There is the love we have for friends, and there is selfless love where we love those who don't love us back. The seeds for all these types of love are planted in our soul when we arrive on this planet and they mature with time. Others can ignite our capacity to love, but they do not put love in us. We received the gift of love on the day we received the gift of life; and that's when we also received our gifts of joy and peace. What if we could love everyone we meet? Wouldn't that provide us great joy?

Our Soul – Love, Joy and Peace

Love, joy and peace are the building blocks of our soul; they are infused into us at birth. They are the foundation of our spiritual center. They are the energy life source inside all of us that we call our spirit, or soul. There is no doubt it exists: the evidence is that we are alive.

The scientific community is in agreement that a force of some kind gives us life; but there is great disagreement about what that force is, because they have yet to discover it. They can understand almost every aspect of our body, but they can't pull out and examine the thing that gives us life – our soul.

That's because our soul does not exist in the physical world, but in the spiritual world. The spiritual world is a completely different dimension from the physical world. That's why scientists have not found it. Our soul is in this spiritual dimension, this world of our Creator. It's a place of perfection, a world of purity. However, although our soul is in the spiritual dimension, it is also in the physical world. It has to be to give us life. In other words it is in both dimensions simultaneously. And if that's true, then it's also a gateway or portal into the world of our Creator – a world of love, joy and peace. And we can verify this by simply asking ourselves if we would rather live a life of love, joy and peace, or a life of hate, sadness and turmoil. The fact that we prefer love, joy and peace over other options verifies that we are in touch with, and influenced by, our soul. It tells us our soul is pure and perfect with a connection to our Creator.

The problem is, however, that most of us don't know that this connection is available to us. That's because we've only known our imperfect physical world – a world that has given us our imperfect thinking structure, and a life of imperfection. We were born to imperfect parents, and lived with imperfect siblings, friends, teachers and preachers. Our society's values are imperfect, many times in opposition to the values of our soul. This physical world has lured us into chasing society's values; it's all we've known most of the time.

So how do we go back to living according to the values of our soul? We do it by redesigning our thinking around the values of love, joy and peace – we redesign it around our soul.

Love Everyone: What if we could love or accept everyone? If so, our joy would certainly increase. Even though some people are difficult to love, there are ways to redesign our thinking structure so we can at least accept them.

Accept Everything: We can accept all that happens. Things happen all the time. But we don't have to judge them good or bad; we can accept them just as they are. That is not to say we can't change things if necessary; we can. But if we let happenings upset us, then our emotions get involved and emotions make poor decisions. If we can keep from battling the negative things that happen, we will make better decisions should changes be necessary.

Enjoy Every Moment: We can enjoy the moment. Our thinking goes on endlessly. It dwells on the past or worries about the future, and we fail to enjoy the moment we are in. As we redesign our thinking, we will discover ways to enjoy all the moments of our lives. When we can love or accept everyone, accept all things that happen and enjoy every moment, then we will be aligned with our soul.

Society tries to lure us into chasing society's values. But we have a free will, and can seek greater values, the values at the center of our being, the values of our soul. When we seek love, joy and peace, we live the life our Creator lives.

Enjoying the Present Moment

The present moment is the field on which the game of life is played. It cannot happen anywhere else. We cannot wait until later to enjoy the present moment, because the present moment is happening now. If we could speak with our spirit, it would encourage us to enjoy the moment. But with our never ending mental chatter, and our overactive lives, we rarely know the present moment is here.

If we want to align ourselves with our souls, we need to be aware that we exist at this present moment; that this moment is here and we can live it to the max. If we are chewing on some past problem or worried about a future difficulty, then we are aligned with useless chatter, and we fail to enjoy the moment. This idle chatter pops up somewhat automatically and is the reason joy is a rare occurrence in many lives today.

<u>Happiness</u>

Life is impermanent. Few things can be depended upon. Relationships dissolve; physical assets depreciate and fall away; and good things and bad things happen to us every day.

It is human nature to try to make good things happen so that we will be happy. But, in fact, the worse place to look for happiness is in things happening. That's because good things don't always happen, and sometimes bad things do. Also, a happening that seems good now might turn out to be terrible later. The student who was elated when he received a motorcycle for graduation was disabled on the new toy two weeks later. Only time can tell if a happening is good or bad.

But we don't need to have good things happen for us to be happy, because the potential for happiness is within us; it's when we align ourselves with the love in our spiritual center. When we do, we stop judging things good or bad, and we find joy and peace in all things that happen.

Our Present Thinking System

Have we ever evaluated our present thinking system, the one that life gave us? Probably not. Let's ask ourselves a few questions. Do we normally find ourselves in a happy, hopeful mood, or do we more often feel sad, discouraged, angry, worried or frustrated? Are we making good decisions and setting good goals for our lives? Or is our life a constant struggle? How would we rate our happiness? On a scale of 1 to 10, with 1 being depressed, 5 being neutral and 10 being joyous, how would we rate our general mood? Sadly, most people rate themselves a 4 or 5. But we don't have to continue at that rating; we can bring more joy into our lives and move our happiness up to a 6 or 7. We can do that by rebuilding our thinking system.

Please know that when we talk about thinking systems, we are not talking about intelligence; we are talking about happiness. Intelligence is understanding big words or figuring out complicated math formulas. People who can do those things can also be suffering with a 3 or 4 happiness level just like anyone else. No, we're talking about happiness. Anyone at any level of intelligence can improve their happiness.

If we had a choice at birth whether we would live life with a happiness level of 4 or 7, we would probably have chosen a 7. But we didn't get that choice back then, so it's not our fault if our happiness level is low. But it is our fault if we don't try to change it – because today we do have a choice. We can make that choice right now. We can say, "Hey, wait a minute. I don't want to continue with this old thinking system given to me by life. I can rebuild my thinking structure into what I want it to be;

and I'm going to do that – I'm going to start right this minute."

Most of us, who have worked on changing our thinking systems, have been able to improve our happiness level as much as 2 points in just a few months. But this kind of rebuilding takes a lot of work. Our old thinking system is in a bad habit of poor thinking, and habits are hard to change.

When we start building our new system, we will often fall back into our old system, because it's all we have ever used to think with. So we will need to work on our new system every hour of every day for months until it becomes our normal way of thinking. Our work will be a series of successes and setbacks. If we focus on our thinking we will think in a new way, but the minute we let our mind drift, we will fall back into our old system. This series of successes and setbacks is normal in the beginning. But the more we work at it, the longer we will remain thinking in the new way. Eventually we will spend most of our time in our new thinking and only revert back to our old system once in a while. Our new system will become a good habit, and our level of happiness will increase.

There's no reason we can't start building our new thinking system right now. There is no one stopping us except ourselves. And a good way to start is by understanding the importance of the present moment.

Surrendering to the Present Moment

If we can accept the world just as it is, we can be at peace with whatever happens. This doesn't mean we don't bring about change when needed. On the contrary, if we accept things, it is easier to effect change than if we battle against them. If we can join into things that at first appear negative, we are better positioned to improve them. Is the present moment of life our friend? Is it an obstacle? Is it an enemy?

If we choose friend, we will welcome whatever is happening in that moment. As we practice making each moment our friend, then over time it becomes a natural way to live. If the present moment is an obstacle, then it's a problem to be overcome, and can trigger negative emotions of impatience, and frustration. If the present moment is our enemy, we will feel we are at war with life. We will hate what we are doing, complain about our surroundings, and curse our situation.

Accepting what happens puts us in alignment with the world and with our soul. Resisting what happens drags out negative emotions. Everything physical is fleeting – things, bodies, events, drama, thoughts, emotions, desires, ambition, fears. They come, pretend to be all-important, and then they are gone, dissolved into the nothingness from which they came. Can we remember yesterday's biggest problem? Was it even real? Who can say?

Our relationship with the present moment is our relationship with life. If the present moment is our friend, then life is good.

There's a saying, "Don't sweat the small stuff." What's small stuff? Everything!

<u>Eliminating Time</u>

In order to be a friend of the present moment we need to eliminate psychological time from our thinking.

We are not eliminating clock time, but the concept of time; the mind's preoccupation with past and future. We need to break our habit of being unwilling to accept whatever is going on in the present moment. If we accept the present moment, just as it is, we dissolve psychological time.

Crazy as it may seem, our subconscious believes something in the future is more important to us than what we are doing right now. Rarely are we totally happy with what we are doing at this moment. When we make peace with the present moment, mental time dissolves, and we can enjoy this moment of our life.

When we can eliminate psychological time, we have a much better chance of being in alignment with our soul. Although our soul exists within our bodies, it simultaneously exists in the spiritual world, a dimension where time does not exist. When we enjoy the present moment, we move closer to our soul and discover our inner peace. But enjoying the moment doesn't mean stopping everything we are doing. It means making our attitude more important than what we are doing. We can experience peace and joy while washing the dishes.

Exercise – Enjoying the Present Moment

With our eyes closed and bodies relaxed we try to feel our eyes – try to be aware of them. Once we feel them, we can relax them. Next, with our eyes relaxed, we try to feel love. We think about the person we love most in the world and we try to feel that love intensely. Then while we are relaxed, and enjoying the positive feeling of love, we can try to feel good about everyone in the world.

So we start by relaxing our eyes, then we try to feel love for the person we love most, then we try to feel positive toward everyone in the world. OK, start.

This exercise is one way we can enjoy the present moment. It only takes a few seconds, and if we practice it every hour, our joy will certainly increase.

Also, we can do a "mindset" exercise. Before we get out of bed or do any activity, we can say to ourselves, "I will love or accept everyone, I will accept all things, I will enjoy this moment." If we can repeat this throughout the day, our new thinking will be in control.

<u>Negative Memories</u>

The statement, "I think," implies we have a say in the matter; that there is choice involved on our part. But many times we no more have a choice in our thinking than in our digestion. Our thinking can go on without our consent, with endless thoughts running through our head. It's a non-stop mental voice that has a will of its own. And because our mind is conditioned by the past, we are forced to reenact the past again and again.

The past lives in us as memories, many of which are of negative events. We often drag out these hurtful remembrances for our mental mastication machine to chew on. Attached to these painful memories are painful emotions. We can choose to dwell on them and suffer the feelings they stir up, or we can bring ourselves back into the present moment and enjoy life. Is thinking about past events worth reducing our happiness? Of course not; it serves no useful purpose. Here are some ways we can stop this useless thinking.

Tragedies

Every life has its tragedies. Moms and dads pass away, siblings die early, parents lose children, fatal accidents and illnesses strike without warning and parents abuse and abandon their children. Tragedies happen; some are inevitable and outside human control. We can choose to let them permanently injure our well being, or we can choose to use them to remind us how short and fleeting life is. The latter will make it easier for us to get back to enjoying the present moment.

Forgiveness

Life is too complicated for anyone to get through it without making mistakes. We have made mistakes, and others have been hurt. Others have made mistakes, and we have been hurt. "Un-forgiveness" is like an emotional acid inside us burning away at our happiness. If we ever expect to have peace in our lives, we need to make forgiveness a major part of our new way of thinking. The sad fact is that many times the worst hurts we have received and given are to those people we love the most. We need to forgive those who have hurt us and we need to ask for forgiveness from those we have hurt.

Nothing good can come from holding on to resentments, grudges or hatreds. Forgiveness makes it possible to remove them. If someone has hurt us, we can bring out the actual hurt and look at it closely. We can ask ourselves if holding a grudge is more important than being happy. If the answer is no, then it is time to forgive those who have hurt us.

Also, it's important to place **our** name on the list of people to forgive, because nothing good can come from holding on to the guilt and shame of old mistakes and failures. Many times it can be harder to forgive ourselves than to forgive others, but we will never fully enjoy life if we can't forgive ourselves. Also, it's easier to forgive ourselves if we can forgive others – and vice versa. Forgiving others can be a way of making amends for the hurts we have caused.

We can make forgiveness a day by day process when we are trying to forgive life's biggest injuries. If we spend a little time on them each day, over time, the negative feelings will diminish.

If we can make forgiveness a major building block of our new way of thinking, our happiness will increase significantly. No one is perfect, not us, not others. Let's make peace with everyone. "I forgive you; please forgive me." It's time to let go of all our ugly resentments, anger, guilt, and shame.

Exercise – Good-by Unhappiness

If a negative memory or emotion won't go away, we should stop and fully face it. We should look at it for what it is, and deal with it. Here is an exercise that will help us to do that. It can free us from negative memories and emotions.

Let's say we are unhappy. The first thing we can do is tell ourselves that unhappiness is an emotion, nothing more. It is not who we are, it is only an emotion we are feeling at this moment. Next we can accept the idea that it is OK to be unhappy. This may seem strange, but fighting against unhappiness won't make it go away, it will only add frustration. So it's important for us to accept our unhappiness. Then we try to feel it; we simply close our eyes and try to intently feel our unhappiness.

Then we try to estimate its intensity and give it a rating; with 1 being miserably depressed to 5 being slightly sad. Let's say we rate it a 3. The next step might sound crazy, but we try to increase our unhappiness; we try to feel even more unhappy; we try to get it down to a 2 or a 1.

You might think this is counterproductive, but the goal is to look at unhappiness objectively and identify it for what it is, an emotion. When we do, we will see that it has not taken over our life, even though it may feel that way. When we feel it and rate it and try to intensify it, it's like holding it up to the light where we see that it is just an ordinary emotion, and we can put it in its place with our other emotions. If we can look at our emotions in this way, we will be able to see that unhappiness is not "who we are," it's only a feeling we are having at the moment. When we can see it in this light, it can't control us or overwhelm us or consumes us anymore. So it is OK to accept our unhappiness, to feel it intently, to give it a rating and try to make it worse. This is all part of seeing it objectively, and shrinking it back down to its real size.

Many of us in our unhappy state, trying to make ourselves even more unhappy, started laughing at ourselves. Our unhappiness had seemed so serious, but the exercise woke us up to how unserious it actually was. We laughed at ourselves because our thinking was so silly, so off base; and life was much less serious than we were making it out to be.

Not only can we use this exercise on our unhappiness, we can also use it to forgive others. We simply accept the hurt we received, feel it intently, give it a rating and try to make it worse. Yes, we try to feel even more hurt than we actually were. If we can do this, there is a good probability our hurt will diminish and forgiveness will come.

This exercise confirms that facing and dealing with our negative emotions can have very positive results. Negative thoughts and memories serve no useful purpose. When we laugh at ourselves, our feelings of hurt diminish, our spirits lift, we lighten up on life, and we can enjoy the moment.

Exercise – Breaking Free

If we really want to feel good – to feel really free, we can do an inventory and house-cleaning of all our hurtful feelings. We can take out and examine all the painful events that happened in our past. We can try to re-feel intently all the original negative emotions, and we can accept them for what they are, emotions. Then we can try to increase their intensity. If someone hurt us, we can try to feel even more hurt. If someone shamed us, we can try to feel even more ashamed, and so forth. The more we try to exaggerate these feelings, the quicker we will see them in an objective light and the faster we will clean them out of our memory. Life is too short to wallow around in old emotions. They serve no useful purpose. We can throw them away.

The Misdirected Thinking of the Ego

The main dysfunction inherent in the human condition is that we miss the point of our existence; which is happiness. Most of us have not achieved full happiness because much of our thinking is negative and our lives are overloaded with activities. Instead of slowing down our hectic pace and enjoying life in the present moment, we worry and work hard so we will be happy sometime in the future. But when that future day arrives we find ourselves driven to continue working, looking to some day further in the future that we will be happy. What is wrong with this picture? Why can't we stop this demanding existence and enjoy life now? The answer is – ego.

Our ego worries about the way the world sees us, so it drives us to create a good public image. Our ego is more concerned with image than with happiness, that's why it's so hard to be happy.

Our ego identifies us with things in our world, such as families, profession, religion, ethnicity, possessions, shape, size and age. It identifies us with our successes and failures; all the things that affect our image. Also, our ego measures our image by the priorities of our society, which are success and possessions. Our ego compares our image to the image of others, and since there are very successful people in the world, this comparison makes us feel like we don't measure up.

The ego's obsession with image is the major flaw in the human thinking system. It diminishes our self-worth, increases our workload and puts any attempt at finding happiness on the back burner. We all want to be happy, yet our ego drives us to expend most of our resources on our image.

The Drives of Our Ego

Sometimes our ego drives us so hard that we start to think that the things that create our image are a part of us. Therefore, if they're lost or damaged we're devastated. If our house is burgled, we feel violated. If our car is stolen, we feel a part of us has been stolen.

Also, our ego has no value system. It will encourage us to do whatever necessary to enhance and/or protect our image, including lying, cheating, stealing and even being violent.

For example, our ego drives us to be successful; therefore it pushes us to do whatever necessary to get a job. Since we need to show our potential employer we are hard working, dependable and skilled, our ego may encourage us to create false references or to lie to get the job. To our ego, success is everything; values are not considered.

Let's say we get the job. Now we will need a car to get to the job. The salesman shows us a medium priced conservative used car we can afford. But he also shows us an expensive new red convertible. Our ego gives high priority to image and low priority to financial responsibility. So if we don't realize our ego is trying to influence us, we will probably buy a car we can't afford.

Let's say we buy the new red car and show it off to all our friends. We look successful and our image soars. But what if we can't make the large car payments? What do we do? If the finance company takes the car, our credit will be destroyed and all we'll be able to afford is an old clunker. We can't even imagine letting our friends see us in an old jalopy after showing off the new red car. This will be a severe blow to our image and our feelings.

Our ego has no relationship with common sense. It will drag us into things that are good for our image without any concern for the consequences.

Ego is Never Satisfied

If our lives are fairly secure, meaning we have a steady job to buy necessities, and a security net of family and friends in the picture, we are in a position to enjoy life, and we can focus on happiness. But our ego is never satisfied with status quo when a possibility arises to enhance our image. For example, we are offered a new job with higher pay, but it comes with more work and more responsibilities. More pay means a bigger house, nicer car, enhanced image. But our happiness, fulfillment and peace will surely decrease because of the longer hours and increased stress? Our ego will make it difficult for us to turn down the higher paying job, even though our happiness will suffer.

If there is one thing we could give to our children we would probably choose happiness. But the example above shows why our ego rarely allows us to choose happiness for ourselves. It is always sending us out to tackle more possessions, more responsibility, and more of anything else that can contribute to our image. Our ego's obsession with image is the major flaw in our thinking system.

The Ego Versus the Real Us

Often our ego focuses on past mistakes and failures because it worries we might make the same mistake again. It spends much more time worrying about past failures than past successes, because failures affect our image far more than successes.

The ego's focus on failures can cause us to start believing that the real us is our failures. But the real us is not our failures, it is the love, joy and peace at the center of our soul. The real us is when love drives our actions.

The real us is the sense of peace in the background of our mind as we do our chores, or relate to other people. The real us is the joy we feel when we contemplate the miracle of life. The real us is the love that emanates from our soul and feels kindness towards others. The real us is when love, joy and peace control our daily lives.

The Illusion of Ownership

If we were on our deathbed with only a few hours left to live, the things we own would be of little value to us. In the proximity of death, the whole concept of ownership stands revealed as ultimately meaningless. All of humanity knows this to be true at some level of thinking; still, we allow our ego to push us to own lots of "stuff." We may have all the stuff we need, but from the ego's point of view, our image is never good enough. If we get what the ego wants, in a short time it wants more. It wants to "want" more than it wants to "have." If we don't recognize this wanting as the ego, we will never be satisfied with what we have, and be condemned to chasing "stuff" for the rest of our lives. Can we see the insanity of our ego?

Being Right Versus Being Happy

An easy way for our ego to increase our image is to make someone else's image smaller. Our ego does it through criticism and name-calling.

Whenever we feel that we are right and the other person or group is wrong, the ego is probably to blame. Is being right more important than being happy?

If we think we are in the right, we can explain the logic of our thinking. If others agree, fine; if not, that's fine too. If we are at peace with the moment, we will be unaffected whether others agree or not. Peace is always better than the need to be right.

If we feel the need to "succeed" and be "great," we can realize this is a favorite fantasy of the ego. Those of us who throw out our chests and bask in the glory of our "successes" are slaves to the eyes of others. "All glory is fleeting." In ten minutes, our egos will be demanding a new success; and many more happy moments will come and go without us. Real success is enjoying the present moment; it's when our actions are in sync with our soul.

Example – Ego at the Wheel

A delivery van driver in the far right lane needed to cross two lanes of traffic to get into the left turn lane. He saw a small opening, turned on his directional signal and started changing lanes. The driver in the first lane slowed down and let him cross, but the driver in the left lane, a teenager, tried to speed up and block him out. The van got in the left lane first, and the teen had to hit his brakes to avoid a collision.

The teen leaned on his horn, shouted insults, and ranted and raved. He had allowed his ego to destroy his emotions. If he had been having a good day, he wasn't anymore. "That's my lane, you can't have it." Using 'me' and 'mine' is the ego doing our thinking for us. "I'm right and he's wrong." That's also the ego.

The driver in the first lane had aligned his thoughts with his soul and allowed and assisted the van in crossing. When we love everyone, accept everything and enjoy the moment, life is good.

Exercise – Identify Ego Driven Behavior

Here are some ego driven behaviors: Becoming worried or anxious; Being tempted to break the rules; Finding ourselves angry or upset over material possessions; Demanding recognition for something we did; Trying to get attention; Bragging about our problems; Making a scene; Giving our opinion when nobody asked for it; Being concerned with how other people see us. Trying to impress others through possessions, knowledge, good looks, status, physical strength, or important people we know; Experiencing anger towards someone or something; Taking things personally; Being offended; Wanting to appear important; Making ourselves right and others wrong.

When we recognize this ego driven behavior, we can defeat it by stopping to enjoy the moment.

Replacing Our Ego With Our Soul

Sooner or later, all of us come to realize that the stress of our hectic life is not normal; it's neither good nor healthy; it's certainly not sane. But society has rarely shown us any other life-style options. Most of us are affected by our ego's insanity to some degree. That's why we need a new way of thinking.

Before we get out of bed, or walk out the door, or start any activity, we can prioritize our thinking. We can think or say our mindset: "Love or accept everyone, accept everything, and enjoy the moment." If throughout the day we can say this before we take any action, then we are thinking in a new way, and our ego will not overpower us.

The real us is not the mental image our ego gives us, but a beautiful spirit at the center of our being.

Therefore, if we can align ourselves with our love, then our joy and peace will increase tremendously.

Our ego drives us to enhance our image; our soul drives us to love and accept others. Our ego creates stress and inadequacy; our soul creates joy and peace. We need to replace our ego's goals with the goals of our soul.

Our ego is always laying in wait, looking for an opportunity to take over our thinking. But it has power over us only if we let it. If we stop regularly to enjoy the moment, if we allow the love in our soul to drive our actions, the ego's power is gone.

Our Inner Purpose and Our Outer Purpose

Our inner purpose is our primary purpose. It's to immerse ourselves in our soul; to submerge ourselves in love, joy and peace – and enjoy the present moment. Our inner purpose is our life long, from birth to death purpose. Our inner purpose is to awaken to the fact that the standard ego-driven lifestyle of possessions and image is insane, and that true happiness is found by being in alignment with our spiritual center.

Our outer purpose is the way we live our physical lives. It is a combination of our relationships, our job, our hobbies and other areas of fulfillment. Our goal is for our outer purpose to always be in sync with our inner purpose.

There is no substitute for finding our true inner purpose – it's not what we do, but who we are. Our inner purpose is to awaken to the need to change the structure of our thinking; to replace our ego's values with our soul's values. Our inner purpose is to surrender to the present moment and all things that happen, even things that at first appear negative. If we see truth in the ideas in this book, it means we are awakening to our inner purpose.

Many of us who are awakening to our inner purpose are no longer certain of our outer purpose. This is good. Now we can find an outer purpose that will be in alignment with our inner purpose.

If what we are doing each moment of our life is the main purpose of our life, we negate time. In doing so we don't worry about past or future. From an emotional point of view, time stands still. We are free to do what we are doing each moment with no pressure or stress, and we can enjoy the moment.

For example, at this moment we are reading this book. If, while we're reading, the thoughts in the background of our mind are that this is the main purpose for our life right now, then we have negated time and we will feel free to read with no pressure or stress. We will be at peace.

On the other hand, if while we are reading this book we are thinking of the next thing we need to do, then clock time is interfering with our present moment, and our enjoyment is diminished.

Time is a paradox. Whatever we do takes time, and yet it is always now. So while our inner purpose is to negate time, our outer purpose involves future, and so could not exist without time. But clock time is always secondary. Whenever we become anxious and stressed, outer purpose has taken over inner purpose. We have forgotten that our state of consciousness is primary, and all else is secondary.

A great man once said, "Yesterday is history, tomorrow is a mystery, but this moment is a gift from the Creator of the Universe." We can't earn this moment, it's a divine gift. When we think in a new way, we enjoy the wonderful gift of this moment. But if we let this moment slip away, we'll never have an opportunity to enjoy it again.

Outer Purpose

The more we align ourselves with our inner purpose, the more our outer purpose becomes obvious. Our outer purpose varies from person to person. No outer purpose lasts forever; it is subject to time and then replaced by a new outer purpose. We may continue doing what we have been doing, only doing it better; or we may make a complete change in our work and/or our living situation. If we change our outer purpose, we may experience uncertainty. This is normal, and if our ego is no longer running our life, we will be comfortable with the uncertainty. We may even find ourselves joyous over the infinite possibilities available to us once the ego's goals are no longer driving our emotions.

Accept the Moment Versus Changing our Life

If we accept the present moment and surrender to whatever life brings, how do we take action; how do we ever make a change in our life or give ourselves a new outer purpose? It depends on what is encouraging our life change; our inner purpose or our ego. Is the change driven by fear and wanting? Are we surrendering to our selfishness? Does the change bring more possessions, work and stress? If so, then our ego is probably driving the change.

On the other hand, if the change will help simplify and unburden our lives; if it will reduce stress and be as good for us as for others, then the change is probably part of our inner purpose.

Three Modalities

If we align ourselves with our soul, we should find ourselves experiencing one of these three emotional states: acceptance, enjoyment or enthusiasm.

Acceptance

Whenever we cannot enjoy what we are doing, we can at least accept it. It will be difficult to enjoy changing a flat tire in the rain, let alone be enthusiastic about it, but we can bring acceptance to it. We can tell ourselves to slow down and accept the moment. We can be at peace with it, "That's alright, these things happen." We can surrender to the situation and realize that it is OK for a tire to go flat.

Enjoyment

When we enjoy what we are doing we feel a sense of aliveness within us. If we are at peace with the present moment, it will be much easier for us to enjoy it. We can relax and enjoy reading this book.

Joy does not come from what we do; it flows into what we do by the way we do it. Joy is a deep sense of aliveness that flows into every action. Before starting any task, we can stop and encourage ourselves to do the best we can – to enjoy what we are doing – to treat it as a hobby.

We can give a gift to a loved-one by taking over a tedious task. For example, we can do dishes for our spouse. If we see this action as giving a gift, it becomes enjoyable. We can discover that our main purpose in life is bringing joy to others. Gandhi said that happiness is found in endeavoring to make the lives of others happy.

If there is a task that we do regularly, like mowing the lawn or taking out the garbage, we can encourage ourselves to relax and enjoy the work. If we put our best effort into it, we will find enjoyment in the task, and discover that whatever we are doing can be enjoyable. If we try to be the most courteous driver on the road we will discover we are the happiest driver on the road.

It is not what we do, but how we do what we do that brings enjoyment. If the main purpose of what we do is the doing itself, then we will enjoy it.

Enthusiasm

One day we may know what our outer purpose is. We may have a vision of a great goal, and awaken to the joy of enthusiasm. Enthusiasm is the deep enjoyment in what we do, plus a goal or vision that we work toward.

Unlike ego driven goals, enthusiasm has high energy and resonates with creative power. Enthusiasm never opposes, it does not confront. It does not create winners and losers, it is based on inclusion; everyone's a winner. It does not need to manipulate people. When enthusiasm encounters obstacles it never attacks, but embraces opposing forces, and turns foe into friend. Enthusiasm knows where it is going, but at the same time it is deeply at peace with the present moment. Enthusiasm wants nothing. Through enthusiasm we enter into full alignment with the Creator of the universe.

Enjoyable Work

If we decide to rebuild our thinking system, the rebuilding will take time. But that's OK, because every moment we are consciously building our system we are living in the present moment and experiencing joy and peace. Yes, it will be a lot of work, but every moment of that work will be enjoyable.

Utopia

Many people hope the world will enter into Utopia someday. But someday means future, and future is just a thought in our mind.

We don't have to wait for Utopia, because it is already inside us. When we think in a new way, we align ourselves with our souls. Then we are driven by love, and our goals are joy and peace. The realization that joy and peace only happen in this moment awakens us to this new way of thinking.

To love is to recognize ourselves in another. Our longing for love is the longing to be recognized, not for what we are, but for who we are. And at our core all humans are the same; we are love, joy and peace.

Love is not love until we give it away. The more love we give, the more we have.

Love is both the weakest force and the greatest force. Love is the weakest force because it can do nothing except by consent. It is the greatest force because it alone can break through the impenetrable fortress known as the hardened human heart.

What can be better than a life based on love?

Mantra

Love everyone, accept everything, enjoy every moment. Our state of mind is more important then what we are doing.

(Many of the ideas in this section are from Eckhart Tolle's book, "The Power of Now.") 1-23-12

Overcoming Depression

In order to overcome depression, we need to maintain a positive attitude. But the very nature of depression drains us of our drive, our hope and our energy. Therefore, overcoming depression won't be quick or easy. But we do have some control – even if our depression is severe and stubbornly persistent.

We can make a huge dent in our depression with simple lifestyle changes: exercising every day, avoiding the urge to isolate, challenging the negative voices in our head, eating healthy food instead of the junk we crave, and carving out time for rest and relaxation. Feeling better takes time, but we can get there if we make positive choices for ourselves each day and draw on the support of others.

Road to Recovery

Recovering from depression requires action. But taking action when we're depressed is hard. In fact, just thinking about the things we should do to feel better, like going for a walk or spending time with friends can be exhausting. It's the Catch-22 of depression recovery. The things that help the most are the things that are most difficult to do. But there's a difference between difficult and impossible.

Start small and stay focused

The key to depression recovery is to start with a few small goals and slowly build from there. We can draw upon whatever resources we have. We may not have much energy, but we probably have enough to take a short walk around the block or pick up the phone to call a loved one.

We can take things one day at a time and reward ourselves for each accomplishment. The steps may seem small, but they'll quickly add up. And for all the energy we put into our depression recovery, we'll get back much more in return.

Step 1: Cultivate Supportive Relationships

Getting the support we need plays a big role in lifting the fog of depression and keeping it away. On our own, it can be difficult to maintain perspective and sustain the effort required to beat depression. The very nature of depression makes it difficult to reach out for help. However, isolation and loneliness make depression even worse, so maintaining our close relationships and social activities are important.

The thought of reaching out to even close family members and friends can seem overwhelming. We may feel ashamed, too exhausted to talk, or guilty for neglecting the relationship. We can remind ourselves that this is the depression talking and that our loved ones care about us and want to help.

- We can turn to trusted friends and family members. We can share what we're going through with the people we love and trust. We can ask for the help and support we need. We may have retreated from our most treasured relationships, but they can get us through this tough time.
- We can try to keep up with social activities even if we don't feel like it. When we're depressed, it feels more comfortable to retreat into our shell.

But being around other people will make us feel less depressed.
- We can join a support group for depression. Being with others who are dealing with depression can go a long way in reducing our sense of isolation. We can also encourage each other, give and receive advice on how to cope, and share our experiences.
- **Pets Can Make Us Happier and Healthier:** While nothing can replace the human connection, pets can bring joy and companionship into our life and help us feel less isolated. Caring for a pet can also get us outside of ourselves and give us a sense of being needed—both powerful antidotes to depression. And the research backs it up. Studies show that pet owners are less likely to suffer from depression or get overwhelmed by stress.

Step 2: Take Care of Ourselves

In order to overcome depression, we have to nurture ourselves. This includes making time for things we enjoy, asking for help from others, setting limits on what we're able to do, adopting healthy habits, and scheduling fun activities into our day.

Do things we enjoy (or used to)

While we can't force ourselves to have fun or experience pleasure, we can choose to do things that we used to enjoy. We can pick up a former hobby or a sport we used to like. We can express ourselves creatively through music, art, or writing. We can go out with friends or take a day trip to a museum, the mountains, or the ballpark.

Develop a Wellness Toolbox

We can come up with a list of things that we can do for a quick mood boost. We can include any strategies, activities, or skills that have helped in the past. The more "tools" we have for coping with depression, the better. We can try and implement a few of these ideas each day, even if we're feeling good.

We can Read a good book.	Listen to music.
List our good points.	Take care of a few tasks.
Watch a funny movie.	Play with a pet.
Take a long, hot bath.	Write in our journal.
Spend time in nature.	Do something spontaneous.

We can push ourselves to do things, even when we don't feel like it. We might be surprised at how much better we feel once we're out in the world. Even if our depression doesn't lift immediately, we'll gradually feel more upbeat and energetic as we make time for fun activities.

Adopt healthy lifestyle habits
- We can aim for 8 hours of sleep. Depression typically involves sleep problems. Whether we're sleeping too little or too much, our mood suffers. We can get on a better sleep schedule by <u>learning healthy sleep habits</u>.
- We can expose ourselves to a little sunlight every day. Lack of sunlight can make depression worse. We can make sure we're getting enough. We can

take a short walk outdoors, have our coffee outside, enjoy an al fresco meal, people-watch on a park bench, or sit out in the garden.
- We can practice relaxation techniques. A daily <u>relaxation practice</u> can help relieve symptoms of depression, reduce stress, and boost feelings of joy and well-being. We can try yoga, deep breathing, progressive muscle relaxation, or meditation.
- We can fight depression by managing stress. Not only does stress prolong and worsen depression, but it can also trigger it. In order to get over depression and stay well, it's essential we learn to <u>minimize and cope with stress</u>.
- We can identify our stressors and figure out all the things in our life that are stressing us out. Examples include: work overload, unsupportive relationships, substance abuse, taking on too much, or health problems. Once we've identified our stressors, we can make a plan to avoid them or minimize their impact.
- We can go easy on ourselves. Many of us are perfectionists, holding ourselves to impossibly high standards and then beating ourselves up when we fail to meet them. We can battle this source of self-imposed stress by challenging our negative ways of thinking.
- We can plan ahead. If we know our stress triggers and limits, we will be able to identify and avoid many landmines. If we sense trouble ahead, we can protect ourselves by dipping into our wellness toolbox and saying "no" to added responsibility.

Step 3: Get regular exercise

When we're depressed, exercising may be the last thing we feel like doing. But exercise is a powerful tool for dealing with depression. In fact, studies show that **regular exercise can be as effective as antidepressant medication** at increasing energy levels and decreasing feelings of fatigue.

Scientists haven't figured out exactly why exercise is such a potent antidepressant, but evidence suggests that physical activity increases mood-enhancing neurotransmitters in the brain, raises endorphins, reduces stress, and relieves muscle tension - all things that can have a positive effect on depression.

To get the most benefit, we should aim for 30 minutes of exercise per day. But we can start small. Short 10-minute bursts of activity can have a positive effect on our mood. Here are a few easy ways to get moving:

- Take the stairs rather than the elevator
- Park our car in the farthest spot in the lot
- Take our dog for a walk
- Pair up with an exercise partner
- Walk while we're talking on the phone

As a next step, we can try incorporating walks or some other enjoyable, easy form of exercise into our daily routine. The key is to pick an activity we enjoy, so we're more likely to keep up with it.

Exercise as an Antidepressant

The following exercise tips offer a powerful prescription for boosting mood:

- We can exercise a little now...and a little more later. A 10-minute walk can improve our mood for two hours. The key to sustaining these benefits is to exercise regularly and often.
- We can choose activities that are moderately intense. Aerobic exercise undoubtedly has mental health benefits, but we don't need to sweat strenuously to see results.
- We can find exercises that are continuous and rhythmic (rather than intermittent). Walking, swimming, dancing, stationery biking, and yoga are good choices.
- We can add a mind-body element. Activities such as yoga and tai chi rest our mind and pump up our energy. We can also add a meditative element to walking or swimming by repeating a mantra (a word or phrase) as we move.
- It's good to start slowly, and not overdo it. More isn't better. Athletes who over train find their moods drop rather than lift.

Step 4: Eat a healthy, mood-boosting diet

What we eat has a direct impact on the way we feel. Aim for a balanced diet of protein, complex carbohydrates, fruits and vegetables. Food is a potent chemical.

- We don't want to neglect breakfast. A solid breakfast provides energy for the day.
- We don't want to skip meals. Going too long between meals can make us feel irritable and

- tired, so we can aim to eat something at least every 3-4 hours.
- We can minimize sugar and refined carbs. We may crave sugary snacks, baked goods, or comfort foods such as pasta or French fries. But these "feel-good" foods quickly lead to a crash in mood and energy.
- We can focus on complex carbohydrates. Foods such as baked potatoes, whole-wheat pasta, brown rice, oatmeal, whole grain breads, and bananas can boost serotonin levels without a crash.
- We can boost our B vitamins. Deficiencies in B vitamins such as folic acid and B-12 can trigger depression. To get more, take a B-complex vitamin supplement or eat more citrus fruit, leafy greens, beans, chicken, and eggs.

Practice mindful eating.

We can slow down and pay attention to the full experience of eating - in other words we can enjoy the taste of food. Also, Omega-3 fatty acids play an essential role in giving our mood a big boost. The best sources are fatty fish such as salmon, herring, mackerel, anchovies, sardines, and fish oil supplements. Some people avoid seafood because they worry about mercury or other possible toxins. But most experts agree that the benefits of eating 2 servings a week of cold water fatty fish outweigh the risks.

Step 5: Challenge negative thinking

Depression puts a negative spin on everything, including the way we see ourselves, the situations we encounter, and our expectations for the future. But we can't break out of this pessimistic mind frame by wishful thinking. We need to replace negative thoughts with more balanced thoughts.

Ways to challenge negative thinking:
- We can think outside ourselves. We can ask ourselves what we're thinking about. If we are being hard on ourselves we can encourage ourselves to move into more positive thinking. We can be realistic about our expectations of ourselves.
- We can keep a "negative thought log. Whenever we experience a negative thought, we can jot down the thought in a notebook, and what triggered it. We can review our log when we're in a good mood. We can consider if the negativity was truly warranted. For a second opinion, we can also ask a friend or therapist to go over our log with us.
- We can replace negatives with positives. As we review our negative thought log we can write down something positive for each negative. For instance, "My boss hates me. She gave me this difficult report to complete" could be replaced with, "My boss must have a lot of faith in me to give me so much responsibility."
- We can socialize with positive people and we can notice how they always look at the bright side of

things – even when dealing with challenges. For example how would they deal with losing their job? Would they see it as an opportunity to find a better job? Or even minor challenges, like not being able to find a parking space. Then we can consider how we would react in the same situations. Even if we have to pretend, we can try to adopt their optimism and persistence in the face of difficulty.

Step 6: We can raise our emotional intelligence

Emotions are powerful. They can override our thoughts and profoundly influence our behavior. But if we are emotionally intelligent, we can harness the power of our emotions. Emotional intelligence isn't a safety net that protects us from life's problems. We will all experience difficulties from time to time. And while these are normal parts of life, they can still degrade our emotions. But emotional intelligence gives us the ability to deal with adversities instead of allowing our emotions to make a bad situation worse. Emotional intelligence gives us resilience.

Emotional intelligence gives us the ability to:
- Remain hopeful during challenging and difficult times
- Manage strong feelings and impulses
- Quickly rebound from frustration and disappointment
- Ask for and get support when needed
- Solve problems in positive, creative ways

Emotional intelligence gives us the tools for coping with difficult situations and maintaining a positive outlook. It helps us stay focused, flexible, and creative in bad times as well as good. The capacity to recognize our emotions and express them appropriately helps us avoid getting stuck in depression, anxiety, or other negative mood states.

Step 7: Know when to get additional help

If we find our depression getting worse and worse, we can seek professional help. Needing additional help doesn't mean we're weak. Sometimes the negative thinking in depression can make us feel like we're a lost cause, but depression can be treated and we can feel better!

If we do get professional help we need to continue doing the previous 6 steps. These tips can be part of our treatment plan, speeding our recovery and preventing depression from returning.

(This information on depression is from HELPGUIDE.org)
10-14-11

Made in the USA
San Bernardino, CA
05 March 2017